THIS BOOK
is the property of

John Gordon Hooten

Library

THE
RESTORATION
PRINCIPLE

THE

RESTORATION

ST. LOUIS, MISSOURI

PRINCIPLE

ALFRED T. DeGROOT

THE BETHANY PRESS

To
McGruder Ellis Sadler
Chancellor
Texas Christian University
whose leadership has achieved
the greatest development in
higher education among Disciples
of Christ since the work of
Alexander Campbell

PREFACE

Disciples of Christ, as a religious body, will live or die, prosper or decline, in accordance with what they think and do about the restoration principle. Ignorance of its history and influence in the career of Christianity as a whole, and in the experience of individual denominations that have made it central in their life, is the worst way of looking at the problem.

Legalistic primitivism or restorationism has stunted the spiritual development and limited the growth of scores and scores of prior movements of this kind. The census lists of religious bodies are dotted with the names and revealing statistics of Christian groups that discovered some one or a few of the teachings of the Bible that had been neglected by the major historic communions, and which were then made the grand cause of a new crusade. Some single doctrine, or small group of doctrines, became the sole stock-in-trade of the ambitious enterprise. It is possible to look across the long experience of the church and to estimate that most of these movements have prospered in accordance with the range of their vision. A cramped, or limited, or distorted estimate of the wholeness of Christian faith and life produces a fellowship with the same characteristics. Smug satisfaction with small success then inclines to insulate the little community from the major concerns and currents of life in the church as a whole. Failure to participate in the throbbing processes of the larger body brings a pallor of sickness and a withering of vitality, to the degree of withdrawal.

Disciples of Christ represent one in the large number of restoration movements that have arisen in the long career of the church. Each was set for an emphasis upon a needed and neglected phase of Christian life. The problem of any such group is to understand its place and to assert its function in the program of the whole community of the faithful and, without apology, to continue this witness; but, at the same time, to participate in the ongoing quest of the whole body as it endeavors to set forth Christ to the world. To live unto itself, to cherish only the rediscovery of the neglected item of truth, is to invite the condemnation of history by a self-chosen low aim.

The glory of the restoration principle is discerned when it is defined in essentially spiritual terms. The church will never be without a need to restore its original, pristine, life-giving aims, aspirations, and dreams. In this path we walk in fellowship with our Lord and with all the great souls impelled by him.

A. T. DeGroot

CONTENTS

CHAPTER I

The Idea of Restoration in Vital Religion

Vital religion is the most powerful force in human life. By it men are inspired to do the normally impossible, as the history of asceticism and the present-day bodily mortifications and controls of the holy men of India give witness. Equally awe-inspiring lives of faith and martyrdom have characterized Christians of conviction in every generation. The destiny of empires has been bent around a standard of religious belief. The frail Gandhi acted as a focusing lens for the faith of a people. Hitler's failure was essentially a religious mistake, for God did not make the human race the way the Fuehrer said. Albert Einstein, a lover of freedom, observed that when the revolution came in Germany, he looked first to the universities as its defenders. They were easily silenced. He then looked to

11

the editors of great newspapers, but their formerly flaming editorials were soon gone. He is often quoted as saying:

Only the Church stood squarely across the path of Hitler's campaign for suppressing truth. I never had any special interest in the Church before, but now I feel a great affection and admiration because the Church alone has had the courage and persistence to stand for intellectual truth and moral freedom. I am forced thus to confess that what I once despised I now praise unreservedly.

The empire-shaking and life-changing power of vital religious faith has no finer example than in the career of Asoka whose reign from 264 to 227 B.C. saw his sway extend from Afghanistan to Madras. H. G. Wells said, "He is the only military monarch on record who abandoned warfare after victory."[1] Disgusted by what he saw of the horrors and cruelties of armed strife he vowed to conquer only by the power of his adopted religion, Buddhism, and pursued the commendable course of first subjugating himself to the ethical virtues of the eightfold path to Nirvana. His power and works now blessed and healed instead of breaking and hurting. Crusades for the digging of wells, the planting of trees, the building of hospitals and the growing of medicinal herbs, the performance of charities, the administration of uplift to aborigines and subject peoples, the promotion of education—even for women—and the inculcation of religion characterized his converted life.

Amidst the tens of thousands of names of monarchs that crowd the columns of history, their majesties and graciousness and serenities and royal highnesses and the like, the name of Asoka shines, and shines almost alone, a star. . . . More living men cherish his memory today than have ever heard the names of Constantine or Charlemagne.[2]

But the vital religious convictions of Asoka did not undergird the work of his successors on the throne and in the Buddhist Order which he had embraced, and on this fact our theme in

---

[1]From *An Outline of History*, by H. G. Wells, p. 369. Copyright 1930. Used by permission of G. P. Wells.

[2]*Ibid.*, p. 371.

this volume finds an early illustration. In that prize adventure book, Yuan Chwang's *Life,* recounting his forbidden trip to India, A.D. 629-645, it is shown that

The faith of Buddha which in the days of Asoka, and even so late as Kaniska, was still pure enough to be a noble inspiration, we now discover absolutely lost in a wilderness of preposterous rubbish, a philosophy of endless Buddhas, tales of manifestations and marvels like a Christmas pantomime, immaculate conceptions by six-tusked elephants, charitable princes giving themselves up to be eaten by starving tigresses, temples built over a sacred nail-paring, and the like.[3]

The need for a restoration of the simple and health-giving beneficence of the more primitive faith was demonstrated in that "In competition with this Buddhism, intellectually undermined as it now was and smothered in gilded decoration, Brahmanism was everywhere gaining ground again,"[4] as Yuan Chwang noted with regret.[5]

An institution is but the lengthened shadow of a man. Religions are in each instance the extension of a personal faith. "Religion is force of belief cleansing the inward parts . . . a system of general truths which have the effect of transforming character when they are sincerely held and vividly apprehended," as Whitehead puts it. It is primarily personal, then naturally social. It is "what the individual does with his own solitariness . . . the art and the theory of the internal life of man, so far as it depends on the man himself and on what is permanent in the nature of things." It is because of this that "The great religious conceptions which haunt the imaginations of

---

[3]*Ibid.,* p. 564.

[4]*Ibid.,* p. 565.

[5]Indeed, Gautama the Buddha thought of himself as the founder of a restoration movement. F. L. Woodward's translation entitled *Some Sayings of the Buddha According to the Pali Canon* (New York: Oxford University Press, 1925) quotes him: "Just as if, brethren, a man traveling in a forest . . . should come upon an ancient road . . . and, as he went, should come upon an old time city, a royal city of ancient days, laid out with parks and water tanks. . . . Then suppose, brethren, that this man should tell of his find to the king or royal minister (and say) . . . 'Sire, restore that city'. . . . Even so, brethren, have I seen an ancient Path . . . traversed by the Perfectly Enlightened ones of former times" (p. 63). J. B. Pratt confirms this judgment in *The Pilgrimage of Buddhism* (New York: Macmillan, 1928), when he explains also that a Bodhisattva is a Buddha in embryo, so to speak, a future Buddha on his way to enlightenment who will in due time restore the ancient law.

civilized mankind are scenes of solitariness: Prometheus chained to his rock, Mahomet brooding in the desert, the meditations of the Buddha, the solitary Man on the Cross."[6]

One of the tragedies of our human constitution is that we do not have more than five senses, so that the means of communicating our full and true faith and feeling are inadequate for conveying them at their best. It is because of this that all religions suffer the fate of Christianity, which tends to become the religion about Jesus instead of the religion of Jesus.[7] There is continually the need of restoring the faith *of* the Founder as well as the faith about him. There is vast significance in the fact that down through the centuries the Christian community has given the honored designation of "a Christlike man" only to men of a gentle ethic and childlike faith, such as Saint Francis, Sadhu Sundar Singh, Kagawa, and Schweitzer. Here is basic historic insight and testimony to the real faith *of* Jesus—his revelation of and trust in a way, a means of making life abundant, as best exemplified in his Sermon on the Blessed Life. This was his religion, to which must be added that indefinable "extra" of confidence that God would not permit his chosen one to see death.

Christianity is the shadow cast by that unmatched life. So firm of faith was the Founder in the validity of his principles that it may be said of him, as it was of his Father, that "with him there is no variation or shadow due to change." (James 1:17.) He lived by the exacting principles of love toward ene-

---

[6]From *Religion in the Making*, by Alfred North Whitehead, Chapter I. Copyright 1927. Used by permission of The Macmillan Company.

[7]It is still pertinent and appropriate, even if not being a complete analysis of the Christian faith, to refer to a distinction made years ago beween the religion *of* Jesus and the religion *about* Jesus. As John Knox says in *The Early Church and the Coming Great Church*, while there was "a solid core" of common belief in the apostolic age, subsequent Christological discussion went astray by emphasizing the *person* of Christ rather than the *event* and the *community* (New York: Abingdon Press, 1955). Ira Jay Martin, long an officer of the National Association of Biblical Instructors, published in 1956 a volume entitled *The Faith of Jesus: a Study for Inquiring Christians*, in which this distinction is crucial. Professor Jean-Louis Leuba treats this distinction in his volume, the English title of which is a vague *New Testament Pattern* but the original French of which is a clearer *L'Institution et l'Evenement* (London: Lutterworth Press, 1953). The original tension in Christ (Son of Man, and Son of David) reappears in a charismatic St. Paul over against the Twelve Apostles, then Protestant versus Catholic emphases. There is an excellent reconciliation of the problem of faith-of and faith-in by J. B. Phillips in his discussion of "The Faith-Faculty" in *New Testament Christianity* (London: Hodder & Stoughton, 1956) and a frank facing of it in the section on "The Return to Orthodoxy" in *The Coming Great Church*, by Theodore O. Wedel (New York: The Macmillan Company, 1946).

mies, of prayer in behalf of those despitefully using him, until his final breath.

His successors and disciples, however, make the shadow cast by this noble faith bulge at so many places that the original outline often is unrecognizable. The gentle teacher of Galilee is claimed to be represented by mailed crusaders dealing slaughter and devastation, and by barbarous inquisitors rending the flesh of those whose spirits they cannot teach because they do not even understand them. The vital faith of Jesus about how to have power among people frequently is distorted into a travesty issuing in power over people.

Where did Jesus come upon his ardent optimism of soul that is commonly called his faith in God—except in his Scriptures, the Old Testament? Harry Ranston, commenting on Ecclesiastes 7:10, says:

Eccles. 7:10. "Say not thou, What is the cause that the former days were better than these? for thou dost not ask in wisdom concerning this." Old age is hardly the point here. The complaint of an old man pondering the days of his own prime is not being countered. Rather he is rebuking those who idealize the distant past to the disadvantage of the present. Probably Koheleth had in mind the Hesodian doctrine of the successive ages of mankind— gold, silver, bronze, iron, etc.—with its underlying belief in the progressive deterioration of the human race. He combats this; bad as things are, the world is not worse than it was. In such a word is revealed the essential Jew. Professor Butcher has written (*Some Aspects of the Greek Genius,* p. 162) that in Greek literature of classical times there is no trace of the thought that the human race as a whole, or any single people in it, is advancing towards a divinely appointed goal. On the other hand, the Hebrew mind was intensely optimistic. The thought of progress was never lost; prophecy and apocalyptic both prove that even in the darkest days the conviction of the best days as ahead was consistently held.[8]

Whatever may be the source of the spiritual healthy-mindedness of our Lord, the need of every sensitive disciple is to

[8]From *The Old Testament Wisdom Books,* by Harry Ranston, p. 289. Copyright 1930 by The Epworth Press. Used by permission.

achieve a restoration, a recapture of the faith of the Founder. The spiritual life of any great soul is discontented until it can have the experience which Browning portrayed—

> That's the wise thrush: he sings each song twice over
> Lest you should think he never could recapture
> The first fine careless rapture![9]

We *live* by rapture, by vital belief in the value of something, or several things. This is the gift religion seeks: the restoration of the Founder's vital faith, his rapturous identification with the very heartbeat of the Creator so that the prosaic world is seen to be verily the substance of a kingdom of God, and its events and histories are bathed in color and meaning emanating from the gallery of eternity.

The saving grace of man's religious nature—that which causes some individuals to be termed the very salt of the earth—is his desire to be *at one* with the passion and faith of the Founder. On the part of the Founder himself this grace is so heightened that disciples elevate it into a doctrine of Atonement, with a capital "A," as a life achievement of peculiar and specific significance and conceived to be of universal efficaciousness for changing the nature, or standing, of disciples. This desire to be at one, this urge toward identity, is observable in all religions; it is what the anthropologist would reduce to a culture pattern. Christianity is not obliged to validate its use of the restoration principle when it is observed that other faiths also use it. Granted, as convinced Christians believe, that the religion of Jesus Christ represents a unique revelation of Deity, the Christian religion is strengthened rather than weakened by the knowledge that it shares (at the level of natural revelation) this common principle with all seekers after truth.

What is true of personal religion is doubly so of institutional life. As light and warmth are dissipated the farther they go out into the void from their generating point, so does distance from its origination give a geometrical increase to the problems of

[9]From "Home Thoughts from Abroad."

vital institutional life. It is possible for an institution so to grow and develop and change through the centuries that its descendant organization bears little resemblance to the original parent. By way of illustration we may note an example in a matter of institutional life, the case of church membership. Originally the method of identification with the Christian community was unmistakable and evident, as well as being a vital personal experience for the individual and a formal demonstration of his new relationship. There is almost no disagreement among scholars[10] that the first-century convert to the Christian gospel was an adult who expressed his faith, was baptized by immersion in water, and thus was ushered into the status of church membership. The use of baptism as the formal act of initiation, after the passion of Jesus, was seen as portraying the spiritual experience of death and burial of the old, un-Christian life, and resurrection to the new way of Christ. The early record of the Book of Acts indicates quite plainly how intense was the sense of fellowship among the Christians. It expressed itself, in part, in a far-reaching benevolence and sharing of goods.

How greatly this matter of fellowship and identification with the Christian community has suffered change is known to every informed reader. Church membership today in most instances begins in irresponsible infancy and in multitudes of cases remains impersonal and unclaimed until the time of "last rites." Even when it is more personally and vitally accepted, on the institutional side the originally meaningful forms with their splendid teaching values are scarcely to be recognized in comparison with their origins.

The problem of keeping intact the original meaning, the freshness, and rapture of the faith of the Founder as it is bequeathed from generation to generation is so universal, so applicable to all religions, that it is possible to formulate general rules or principles of development which tend to obtain in the

---

[10]For a recent contribution in this field, see D. M. Baillie, *The Theology of the Sacraments* (New York: Charles Scribner's Sons, 1957). This important late Presbyterian says, "In every part of the New Testament it appears to be assumed that baptism was the universal and essential gate of entry into the Christian community." He discusses the use of immersion, and adds "but all that powerful symbolism seems to disappear when for the immersion we substitute a few drops of water sprinkled on the brow." (Used by permission of Charles Scribner's Sons.)

17

history of any given institution. Each generation is obliged to express its inward faith in terms that are meaningful to itself and understood by the folk of its time—if these folk are to be reached with the message of this faith. When we see how constantly the tendency (indeed, the necessity) of change in outer expression comes to the religious organization, we will at the same time see how vital it is that the changes in expression shall not do violence to its essential message and we will see, also, how valid is the restoration idea, the urge to recapture the true faith and to enjoy and relive the original way.

The course of religions runs in fairly well-defined cycles in this matter of the expression of their original purpose and passion. In the use of formal or ritualistic means for this expression, three stages may be distinguished. They are the periods of (1) obliviousness, (2) balance, and (3) art for art's sake. These phases of religious development in its organized or institutional life may be observed in utmost clarity not only in Christianity but also in other faiths. Such development is not inevitable but is almost certain unless checked by constant reformatory programs. The intensity of the faith of the first disciples who have personal contact with and inspiration from the Founder needs no beauty in its forms; it needs only fitness, or faithful representation of its passion. Artistry is entirely subordinated to feeling and is uncritical of its own form. But when some years have passed, and the new religion moves out into a society which has grown old in its habits and customs, where things are cherished because they are stable and traditional and dependable, because they have roots in antiquity and in fitness made smooth by the wear of the ages, there comes a period of balance in which the formal arts no longer are decried but rather are adopted and used. The object is to give the new faith a more ready acceptance in the eyes of the folk who know religion only as something old and settled and established in its practices. The natural temptation of artistic souls who grow up in the religion when it has been long accepted and traditional is to turn to a contemplation of the art alone. Scholasticism runs rampant while theological hairsplitting and ritualism have what sportsmen call a "field day." The original, life-geared religion of the Founder which was designed to be of a personal, practical, and health-giving nature becomes an involved system, confounded by disputing experts in the study of antiquities, housed in great establishments and jealous of vested interests, with the worship of the humble soul declared invalid unless it pays tribute to a priesthood which has intervened itself between the disciple and his God. It is then that there arises the conviction of many who are intelligent enough to judge a faith by its fruits that religion is the opium of the people, and the watchword of a generation which has been robbed of its individual spiritual birthright becomes *ecrasez l'infame!*—wipe out the infamous thing!

This constant tendency of the forms and ordinances of a religious institution to become mere habit, devoid of the spirit which gave them birth and shape, has a continuing illustration in the instance of a people in the land which was the cradle of the Christ. Lawrence of Arabia tells in his *Seven Pillars of Wisdom* how

The Wahabis, followers of a fanatical Moslem heresy, had imposed their strict rules on easy and civilized Kasim. In Kasim there was but little coffee-hospitality, much prayer and fasting, no tobacco, no artistic dalliance with women, no silk clothes, no gold and silver head-ropes or ornaments. Everything was forcibly pious or forcibly puritanical.[11]

The agriculturally settled and the city-dwelling Arabs could feel that they had followed religion's renunciation of the world while still enjoying such stability and comfort as their ingenuity and labor could cause the earth to provide. Not so the Wahabis—and when they gathered numbers enough, in they would come from their desert homes forcibly to evangelize, to restore and impose their conception of the true life of faith. Says Lawrence:

It was a natural phenomenon, this periodic rise at intervals of little more than a century, of ascetic creeds in Central Arabia. Always the votaries found their neighbours' beliefs cluttered with inessential things, which became impious in the hot imagination

[11]From *Seven Pillars of Wisdom*, by T. E. Lawrence. Copyright by Doubleday & Co., Inc., and used by permission.

of their preachers. Again and again they had arisen, had taken possession, soul and body, of the tribes, and had dashed themselves to pieces on the urban Semites, merchants and concupiscent men of the world. About their comfortable possessions the new creeds ebbed and flowed like the tides or the changing seasons, each movement with the seeds of early death in its excess of rightness.[12]

The history of all continuing religions is a record of recurring restoration programs. In Walter Marshall Horton's volume, *Can Christianity Save Civilization?* there is presented in long array the account of the renewal of these religions by means of refreshment at the springs from which the fathers drank, or by conversion to another system of beliefs.

Such a scholarly array of examples from world history is but a reiteration of the central theme of the historical books of the Old Testament, "Thou shalt have no other gods before me." The falling away of the Hebrew people to Baal worship, or to the adoration of provincial gods—gods of the local hearth and kin, or seasons, of fertility, and of natural forces on which life depended—was a prophecy of man's fatality through small faith, a faith uncertain and weak in its grasp of its grand conception of a universal Jehovah, the One God. As Israel lapsed time after time into the inviting ease of Baalism, with its sanction of and reveling in passion and low aim, she set the pattern for small minds and faint faith ever thereafter, down to the recent recrudescence of nationalistic worship of blood and soil. In between these movements separated in time by more than 3,000 years, but otherwise closely akin, it would be possible to assign to their stations in the calendar of the centuries the brother movements in this fraternity of exclusiveness. From the Philistines until the white citizens councils of today there have been people content to live in the suburbs of henotheism and worship a provincial deity when the city of God with the temple of the universal Father stood open for the forgiveness of sins and the healing of the nations.

---

[12]*Ibid.*

The prophet, however, saved Israel.[13] He restored the worship of the One Father, and provided a hearing community for the coming Messiah. One such prophet was Hezekiah, reforming king of Judah. When he came to the throne (727, 721?), the land was rife with idolatry and Baalism, or nature worship. A most cherished object of worship was the brass snake Moses had made centuries before. Hezekiah demolished the Baal groves and pillars, and destroyed the Mosaic serpent. The people burned incense before it, but Hezekiah called it "a piece of brass." (2 Kings 18:4.) So iconoclastic was this action and Hezekiah's language that the King James translators did not render the Hebrew into English lest common ears be offended; they wrote only, "He called it Nehushtan."

Of like import was the preaching of Jeremiah in the seventh century B.C. Some centuries before, the most holy object of reverence was the ark of the covenant. So wonder-working were its powers and so venerated was its physical presence that we read of the great warrior Joshua that he "rent his clothes, and fell to the earth upon his face before the ark of the LORD until the evening." (Joshua 7:6.) Half a millennium later Jeremiah could say, "And when you have multiplied and increased in the land, in those days, says the LORD, they shall no more say 'the ark of the covenant of the LORD.' It shall not come to mind, or be remembered, or missed; it shall not be made again." (Jeremiah 3:16.) He was of quite a different temper as compared with Ezekiel who, "In his plan of restoration (Ezekiel 40—48), not only took extraordinary precautions to prevent future defilement of the land and people . . . but made of the Temple service the agency for the removal and expiation of all profanations."[14]

No more revolutionary event in religious organization occurred for Judah than when King Josiah in 621 B.C. closed all

---

[13]The prophet does this—not the scholar, though the latter may try, fated as he is to reach with his message only the few with whom religion is mainly a matter of intellect. The author of the *Wisdom of Solomon* made his effort in this field. Living in a day when more primitive tales would not suffice among the learned, his book recast the flood story in immaterial term. It was all an allegory; God was not actually present: he was there only as "Wisdom." The object of this writing was to bring Judaism up to date, and to make God's creative action understandable to philosophers.

[14]From *Introduction to the Old Testament*, by R. H. Pfeiffer, p. 243. Copyright 1941 by Harper & Brothers. Used by permission.

local shrines, called all priests to Jerusalem, and ruled that God could be worshiped with true adequacy only in the capital city and in an institutional and formal manner. An even more revolutionary idea was promulgated centuries later by the greatest prophet, Jesus, who dared to challenge the admittedly pious Josiah with a personal religion by saying, "The hour is coming, and now is, when the true worshipers will worship the Father in spirit and truth, for such the Father seeks to worship him." (John 4:23.)

It is ever the prophet who uncovers and cleanses the flowing springs of enduring religious faith. Through the centuries nations and priesthoods build formal monuments over and around these sources of life and refreshment, exact toll of the pilgrims who ask the way to them, and regulate the groupings in which they may have access to them. When life becomes too miserably cluttered with temples and taboos, a cleansing of the springs from these trappings is essential for true worship. This is the function of that most vital of the advocates of true religion, the restorationist or prophet. He calls back to the health-giving worship of the universal Father headstrong egoists and the erring ignorant. He distinguishes between the essential principles which make for peace and the abundant life well pleasing to the one God, as over against the petty, provincial rules and peculiar customs which small minds would elevate into a *sine qua non* of acceptable worship and way of life. He is not a luxury that can be afforded by a church grown sleek with its balanced diet of variegated ministries—he is rather the indispensable vitamin without which the body in spite of its careful regimen and splendorous dress is found in a fateful moment to lack the vibrant health equal to the demands of a crucial testing hour.

Many a widespread religion grown fat and sluggish has suddenly been confronted by a vigorous, new, crusading community which by war, or commercial expansion, or simply by religious evangelization has penetrated not only the ancient society but also has captured its religious idealism and loyalty through a fresh demonstration of what it means to see the great vision, to behold the exalted throne of the Eternal whence all inspiration to the blessed life issues. A Founder of the faith may serve his

22

day, and cause such a reverberation of the harmonies of human life that its tone lingers on for generations, but the formal musicians in the temple will play by rote and not by inspiration after a time until a true hearer of the harmonies appears among them again—one who has paid the price of disciplined practice but who also has so forgotten self-advantage or the world's remuneration that he is in tune with the Founder and the Founder's Father, the one God. Such a one makes a music lovely to the soul of religion in the common man. It may at the same time be unrecognized by the very music masters who have learned only by rote from progressively uninspired practitioners. But there is an undeniable authority which belongs to the restorer in religion. He reappears in the pages of history because life becomes too unsavory without that which he hears and brings to the people from the source of eternal truth.

We must qualify our judgment about the essential function of the restorer in religion by saying that he *may* serve in the prophetic role. This is his true psychology, for he is fundamentally a searcher after the original element in worship. Faith precedes ritual, and initiates organization. It is only the restorer grown tired who rests on the achievements of his brethren as of a given date and calls them perfection. He becomes a priest, a formalist, a literalist, not remembering that "the letter killeth." He wants to go back to some *thing,* rather than to share always the creative spirit of the Founder, to which all things are but means to an end. And the end or purpose of Christianity is always the reproduction of the kind of life which came into the world in the person and example of Jesus.

In the introduction to his volume, *Saint Francis of Assisi,* Paul Sabatier draws a contrast boldly:

The priest of the thirteenth century is the antithesis of the saint, he is almost always his enemy. Separated by the holy unction from the rest of mankind, inspiring awe as the representative of an all-powerful God, able by a few signs to perform unheard-of mysteries, with a word to change bread to flesh and wine into blood, he appeared as a sort of idol which can do all things for or against you and before which you have only to adore and tremble.

23

The saint, on the contrary, was one whose mission was proclaimed by nothing in his apparel, but whose life and words made themselves felt in all hearts and consciences; he was one who, with no cure of souls in the Church, felt himself suddenly impelled to lift up his voice. The child of the people, he knew all their material and moral woes, and their mysterious echo sounded in his own heart. Like the ancient prophet of Israel, he heard an imperious voice saying to him: "Go and speak to the children of my people!" . . .

These thirteenth-century saints were in fact true prophets. Apostles like St. Paul, not as the result of a canonical consecration, but by the interior order of the Spirit, they were the witnesses of liberty against authority.[15]

What happens to the institution of religion when it sees itself failing as the preserver of the very heartbeat of faith is plain. Sabatier continues:

When the priest sees himself vanquished by the prophet he suddenly changes his method. He takes him under his protection, he introduces his harangues into the sacred canon, he throws over his shoulders the priestly chasuble. The days pass on, the years roll by, and the moment comes when the heedless crowd no longer distinguishes between them, and it ends by believing the prophet to be an emanation of the clergy.

This is one of the bitterest ironies of history.[16]

It is the grand conception of religion to restore the best it has learned about the righteous life to every man who has fallen short of this high calling. Progress can sometimes be made by going backward—when that going backward is to guiding principles. This is not defeatism, nor the worship of an assumed golden age, nor distrust of new and more serviceable programs. Methods and customs are subordinate in value to ideals. But wherever there has been a founder who has shown the way to higher life, there will be need of a program which restores his principles to those who seek the same noble ends.

---

[15]From *Saint Francis of Assisi*, by Paul Sabatier, translated by Louise Seymour Haughton, pp. xiv-xv. Copyright 1894 by Charles Scribner's Sons. Used by permission.
[16]*Ibid.*, p. xv.

CHAPTER II

The Restoration Concept
in the Ante-Nicene Fathers:
Clement to Tertullian

To thee, O Gaudentius, thou choice glory of our doctors, belongs such vigor of mind, yea, such grace of the Spirit, that whatever you say even in the course of your daily preaching, whatever you deliver in the church, ought to be preserved in books, and handed down to posterity for their instruction.

> (Rufinus' introduction to the *Recognitions of Clement,* commending this work to Bishop Gaudentius, perhaps in the first third of the third century.)

Having recognized the necessity in any vital religion of keeping fresh the faith of the Founder, our task now is to see how this need has been supplied in the career of the Christian community. What ways of personal and congregational life were valued by those who lived in times early enough to learn these methods from leaders personally acquainted with the apostles? What attitudes toward a continuing church and Christian society did they sustain, and hence what rules for social living were emphasized? Was fellowship encouraged among the different congregations which had been called into being by the evangelists busy before the age of written scriptures, which reflected and emphasized the special insights and concerns of these men? If so, what common hopes or beliefs or practices were the grounds of this fellowship? Coming to the special theme of this volume, which is the restoration principle as formulated by the Christian Church (Disciples of Christ), with the advent of New Testament scriptures did the early Christians of the Ante-Nicene age look upon these writings as the specifications and diagrammatical outline of an ecclesiastical pattern, an unchangeable church, to which all congregations of apostolic founding and oversight adhered, and to the model or blueprint to which all subsequent (in this case, all Ante-Nicene congregations) churches endeavored to conform? In brief, did the Fathers of this vital period of formative Christian life have in mind, and use, the restoration plea?

A query so basic to the validity of the ideological charter of any restoration movement within the church demands an answer. There are three possibilities before us. (1) If the whole concept of a New Testament pattern church is of purely American origin, in the minds of such leaders as James O'Kelly, Barton W. Stone, Abner Jones, Elias Smith, Thomas and Alexander Campbell, and Walter Scott, their program becomes simply another interesting intellectual emergence in the theological career of the church universal. (2) On the other hand, if the idea of a church always measuring itself by certain revealed standards of doctrine, worship, and behavior ("by express terms or approved precedents") ranged in the mind, and was made vocal and explicit in the writings and organizational activities of the Ante-Nicene leaders, then the restoration program enjoys a historical grounding which cannot rightly be disregarded by the church today even though any particular restoration concept, as formulated in the modern period, was lost to the Christian world for more than a thousand years. (3) If, however, we find in the Fathers a *variegated restorationism,* then the restoration idea enjoys a fundamental validity, but in a fashion vastly different from the rigidity with which it has been proclaimed by much of the preaching of certain communions.

By *variegated restorationism* is meant that several early disciples of the Christian way may have had different points of doctrine, worship, and behavior which they felt to be most vital and helpful in the message of Jesus as communicated by the "apostles, prophets, and teachers."

Our task, then, is to examine the writings of the Ante-Nicene Fathers and discover in what manner they expected to restore the faith of the Founder to his disciples of their day. Vital religion demands precisely this practice. The life-changing power of the Founder's faith must be made available to the new convert. Was there apostolic—and Ante-Nicene—uniformity in the content of this message? Was there, further, apostolic—and Ante-Nicene—uniformity in the type of church organization or polity, order of worship, doctrinal requirements for membership, methods of receiving new adherents, and ways of behavior required for a continuing fellowship, among all these churches? If uniformity in these areas was not everywhere required, what was the basis of the unity of the churches? This last question must wait for its answer until the concluding portions of the volume of which the present treatment is only a part, but the former queries find their replies in those treasured mirrors of the life of the early Christian communities, the works of the Ante-Nicene Fathers.

It may be objected that it is improper to look for the use of the restoration idea in the writings and works of the Ante-Nicene Fathers, because they *already had* the pure Christian faith. In support of this claim it may be argued that they were concerned that the church was and should continue to be apostolic through pure doctrine and sacramental life, as seen in a sacred canon of scripture, a baptismal creed, and a sense of its being the guardian of the tradition.

The answer to this is in the variety of concepts, doctrines, and practices which we shall see the Fathers advocating as this chapter unfolds.[1] Each one hailed the apostles—but made his own selection of the particular apostles and the particular teachings and practices of those apostles which seemed to his reverent judgment as being needed for his day. Apostolicity was a cherished commodity, but selectivity was the process by which

---

[1] See, for example, David Eugene Olsen, *Ante-Nicene Doctrine Departure From New Testament Teaching* (Minneapolis: 1920), 60 pp.

new leaders gave development to a living church. Furthermore, to claim that the Ante-Nicene churches possessed and practiced unmodified, primitive Christianity would be to put the writings of the Fathers practically on a level with the New Testament—which few would be willing to do.

τὰ ἀρχαια 'ἔθη χρατέιτο, "Let the primitive examples prevail," was the slogan and intention of the Christian council at Nicea in the year 325. So important was this council that in Christian history the thought of its first several centuries is by common consent termed Ante-Nicene or Post-Nicene, hinging at the year 325. It was the claim of the council that it did not make any conception into doctrine that was not recognized as such before. The works of the Ante-Nicene Fathers, then, are the materials which should reflect the church's understanding of its primitive faith. These writings are our only self-portrait, today, of the church of the first three centuries. They are the express image of its understanding of itself in its intent and purpose.

Few finer exercises for the increase and strengthening of Christian faith can be engaged in than reading the Ante-Nicene Fathers. Man, made in God's image (Judaism says this can refer only to rational endowment, since God is not corporeal), must have an object for his contemplation. Providence has sprinkled every period of history with great minds, and these masterful intellects have ever sought a system of belief that would challenge their largest competency. It is like occupying the universal reviewing stand of very Deity to take into intimate view the intellectual home-seeking of the great minds of early Christian centuries. Through the pages of the Fathers one may see man at his best, in the divine image, "little lower than God," in noble humility searching for the satisfaction of the interrogative instinct that makes him man. As in a species of planetarium of the mind, here may be seen in short span three centuries of restless intellect in search of its master—and finding it in the Christian faith.

Let us, then, see what elements of the faith of the Founder(s), Jesus Christ—and the apostles, it is significant to note—loomed largest in the instruction of the Fathers.

I

When Clement of Rome wrote his epistle to the Corinthians, about A.D. 97, his purpose was to bring peace in place of the divisions which had so weakened that congregation. Naturally his appeal was for a re-establishment of its former harmony. After noting multiplied examples of the blessings of humility he says, "Wherefore, having so many great and glorious examples set before us, let us turn again to the practice of that peace which from the beginning was the mark set before us."[2] In preaching and kindred admonition unto the good life, what we may call *ethical restorationism* is frequently used. The history of preaching, from the works of the Ante-Nicene Fathers down to the present day, is a constant witness to the value of this homiletical instrument.

To the major portion of I Clement presented in Volume I of the Fathers there is added a reprint and completion of this epistle in Volume IX on the basis of an 11th-century manuscript, discovered at Constantinople in 1875. More than six chapters are added to I Clement, and in this new material the author says:

. . . If, however, any shall disobey the words spoken by Him through us, let them know that they will involve themselves in transgression and serious danger; but we shall be innocent of this sin, and, instant in prayer and supplications, shall desire that the Creator of all preserve unbroken the computed number of his elect. . . .[3]

The "words spoken by Him through us" are as close as this literature comes to the ideas under our investigation, and the "us" is not a reference to the apostles. As A. V. G. Allen points out, Clement lays claim to the prophetic office.[4] Indeed, Mr.

---

[2] First Epistle of Clement to the Corinthians, Chapter XIX. All quotations from *Ante-Nicene Fathers* are from the edition of the Christian Literature Publishing Co. (Buffalo: 1887).

[3] Chapter LIX.

[4] Clement does this in Chapter XL. See A. V. G. Allen, *Christian Institutions* (New York: Scribners, 1910), p. 48.

Allen adds, Clement's purpose apparently was to restore something that Jesus had specifically done away—the distinction between clergy and laity. Clement went only as far as giving a strong analogy of the Christian leadership to the Old Testament priesthood, but Cyprian and others were later to carry his idea to its logical fulfillment.

New material given in the manuscript of 1875 includes Chapters 12-20 of II Clement (the former portion being in Volume VII of this series). In it occurs this sentence:

. . . So, then, brethren, if we do the will of our Father God, we shall be members of the first church, the spiritual—that which was created before sun and moon; but if we shall not do the will of the Lord, we shall come under the Scripture which saith, "my house became a den of robbers."[5]

Here is an instance of a theme that shall be found recurring frequently in the Fathers, what II Clement in the same chapter calls "the church of life," which means the recapturing or restoring of a type of life with fruits in benevolent living deserving of salvation.

II

A species of *mystical restorationism* in which the disciple seeks to recapture for his own life the passion and suffering and total experience of the Founder is of frequent occurrence in the career of early Christianity. Ignatius wrote to the church at Rome en route to his martyrdom there about the year 116 saying:

. . . I beseech of you not to show an unseasonable good will toward me. . . . let fire and the cross; let the crowds of wild beasts; let breakings, tearings, and separation of bones; let cuttings off of members; let bruising to pieces of the whole body; and let the very torment of the devil come upon me: only let me attain to Jesus Christ. . . . Permit me to be an imitator of the passion of Christ, my God.[6]

---

[5] Chapter XIV.
[6] Chapters IV, V, VI.

In the longer version of this letter Ignatius multiplies his longing for identification with the Lord, saying:

. . . Provoke ye greatly the wild beasts that they may be for me a grace and may leave nothing of my body, in order that, when I have fallen to sleep I may not be a burden upon anyone. Then shall I be in truth a disciple of Jesus Christ, when the world seeth not even my body.[7]

In the heights of passion for this mystical sharing of the rapture of the Founder, Paul could estimate himself to have achieved sufficient identity with his Lord that he might "admonish . . . as my beloved children" lesser devotees in the categorical command, "Be imitators of me." (1 Corinthians 4:14, 16.) In a later day a spurious author of the epistle to the Antiochians enjoyed the same mystical union, saying, "Ye have been the disciples of Paul and Peter . . . Be ye followers of me."[8]

III

There is a most intriguing new concept of the restoration plan to be found in Papias (died A.D. 130), a hearer of the apostle John and perhaps acquainted with others who knew Jesus firsthand. Papias says:

. . . But I shall not be unwilling to put down, along with my interpretations, whatsoever instructions I received with care at any time from the elders, and stored up with care in my memory, assuring you at the same time of their truth. For I did not, like the multitude, take pleasure in those who spoke much, but in those who taught the truth; nor in those who related strange commandments, but in those who rehearsed the commandments given by the Lord to faith, and proceeding from truth itself. If, then, any one who had attended on the elders came, I asked minutely after their sayings—what Andrew or Peter said, or what was said by Philip, or Thomas, or by James, or by John or by Matthew, or by any other of the Lord's disciples: which things Aristion and the presbyter John, the disciples of the Lord, say. For I imagined

[7]Chapter IV.
[8]Chapter VII.

that what was to be got from books was not so profitable to me as what came from the living and abiding voice.[9]

This endeavor to restore and to keep alive the testimony of the *vocal* instructions of the primitive church leaders, to the exclusion of other interests, is unique in Papias. New Testament Christianity would not wholly have served his desires; he wanted something more primitive and personal.

Perhaps this claim to uniqueness should be modified by saying that this was true of Papias for Christianity only—for the same opinion emerged just as truly and as naturally in Mohammedanism. Atkins and Braden state:

One may doubt whether Mohammed himself anticipated the absolute authority the Koran has asserted over Islam. He certainly made no attempt to assemble its widely scattered fragments. He did insist on the truth of his own revelations and their authority over his followers, but he may well have had in mind his own living, continuous message and not the deposits of it on leather, bones, and palm leaves.[10]

IV

Justin Martyr, who lived from about A.D. 110 to 165 was a gentile convert to Christianity who became a master of the most intricate details of the Old Testament scripture. He was a philosopher by profession and was perhaps the first Christian to practice philosophy as a means of livelihood. He was devoted to truth as he saw it, even to martyrdom. In his *First Apology* he says, "Reason directs those who are truly pious and philosophical to honor and love only what is true, declining to follow traditional opinions (or, 'the opinions of the ancients') if these be worthless."[11] Thus Justin begins by eulogizing truth and discounting opinions which are merely ancient, and his argument proceeds in a manner designed to restore truth to its proper place in the current legal judgments against the Christians in-

[9]Chapter I, 153.
[10]From *Procession of the Gods*, by G. G. Atkins and C. S. Braden, p. 441. Copyright 1948 by Harper & Brothers. Used by permission.
[11]Chapter II.

stead of condemning them simply because of their bearing a certain name.

If our purpose were to show that Justin conceived of Christianity as the application or restoration of the original, primitive ethic of Jesus, our pages would be burdened with quotations, for his *Apology* is replete with this line of argument. Or, if we desired to show that as a (Christian) philosopher Justin proposed to present Christianity as the revelation through Jesus of truth which had at least been partially perceived by other philosophers, this too could readily be done from his words, e.g., *First Apology,* Chapter XX, "Heathen Analogies to Christian Doctrines."

The reading of the exhaustive writings of Justin on any theme which he handles sets the subject of restorationism in a new perspective. If the idea of a patterned church had been prophesied in the Old Testament or employed in the developing New Testament, the reader is easily persuaded that the martyr would have set it forth with elaborate documentation and comment. He is almost wearisome in his covering of the principal subjects of discussion among the second-century churches. Chapter after chapter is given to the prefiguring by types in the Old Testament of just about everything that comes to pass in the New Testament. The long argument in the *Dialogue* beginning at Chapter XCVIII on the subject of "Predictions of Christ in Psalms XXII"—a psalm which includes the verse,

> I will tell of thy name to my brethren;
> in the midst of the congregation I will praise thee—

carries no mention of the ecclesiastical pattern. Chapter CXXXIV, near the conclusion of the *Dialogue,* entitled "The marriages of Jacob are a figure of the Church," makes no use of this concept. The absence of the idea of the restoration of an ecclesiastical model in Justin is a fact to be reckoned with in our consideration of this theme. His section in the *Dialogue* beginning with Chapter XL which carries his argument in terms of Old Testament types of New Testament developments, lends

33

itself splendidly to the use of the pattern idea—but it is not found there. His specific reference to the church in Chapter XLII carries no suggestion of its being organized on the basis of an unvarying outline.

Justin was a loyal Christian ("I and others who are right minded Christians on all points . . ." *Dialogue,* Chapter LXXX) sustaining a high appreciation of every means of honoring the Christ in whom he trusted for salvation after a long search among the religions of his day. He appreciated the ordinances (see the concluding chapters of the *First Apology*) but did not give to ritual performances or to patterns of organization any religious virtue beyond that of the spirit and attitude which employed them. To Trypho he could say, "What need have I of that other baptism, who have been baptized with the Holy Ghost?"[12]

V

The Epistle of Barnabas (A.D. 100, 150?) was probably written by a Jew whose Maccabean spirit could not but be inflamed by the destruction of Jerusalem by the Roman General Titus in his time. Such an event would in itself suggest to his mind the desirability of some divine scheme for the re-establishment of this city in another, more spiritual or perhaps institutional, fashion. If, as the author claims in Chapter I, "The Lord hath made known to us by the prophets both the things which are past and present, giving us also the first-fruits of the knowledge of things to come," we should expect to find frequently in the pages of this writer the idea of a church patterned on apostolic revelation of its essential norms—providing the idea ever was in his mind.

Barnabas says of the Deity, "He hath made us after another pattern," and quotes the scriptures, "I will confess to Thee in the Church,"[13] but this contiguity of terms does not suggest to him the idea of a pattern of the church. In harmony with the common modes of Christian thought in this era, Barnabas

---

[12]*Dialogue,* Chapter XXIX.
[13]Chapter II.

finds Old Testament types or foreshadowings of the great and even insignificant events of New Testament times in the church. Such habits of thought should aptly suggest the pattern idea of the nature of the church, but one looks in vain for it in his pages. Almost every sentence of Chapter XVI, "The Spiritual Temple of God," could serve as a starting point for introducing the conception. Instead, we find here, as throughout Barnabas, the proclaiming of salvation not by means of institutional devices nor conformity with prearranged ordinances, but by a "trust in the name of the Lord" and "the commands of the doctrine"—which he promptly defines at length in Chapter XVIII, entitled "The Way of Light," a catalog of the Christian personal, ethical virtues.

VI

The march of Christianity to the West through the work of pioneer leaders is represented by Irenaeus of Lyons (120-202) and his treatise, *Against Heresies*. Here is a topic made to order for the bringing forth of any program of Christian life and work in contradistinction to false or heretical organization. Irenaeus is very conscious of "the church"; he refers to it with a frequency new in the Fathers. Book I, Chapter X, under the title "Unity of the Faith of the Church Throughout the Whole World," presents this faith in terms of an outline of beliefs suggestive of the so-called Apostles' Creed. He says:

As I have aready observed, the church, having received this preaching and this faith, although scattered throughout the whole world, yet, as if occupying one house, carefully preserves it. She also believes these points (of doctrine) just as if she had but one soul, and one and the same heart, and she proclaims them, and teaches them, and hands them down, with perfect harmony, as if she possessed only one mouth.

As our reading of the voluminous remains of Irenaeus produces for us no example of his advocacy of an ecclesiastical or organizational type of restorationism, we begin to notice such wisdom as he may have for our study. Much of his Chapter

XXVIII in Book I could have been written for reference to the modern church, for he says:

Many offshoots of numerous heresies have already been formed from those heretics we have described. This arises from the fact that numbers of them—indeed, we may say all—desire themselves to be teachers, and to break off from the particular heresy in which they have been involved. Forming one set of doctrines out of a totally different system of opinions, and then again others from others, they insist upon teaching something new, declaring themselves the inventors of any sort of opinion which they may have been able to call into existence.

If the idea of restoring any phase of New Testament experience which had been lost or neglected was present in the mind of Irenaeus at all, it was a revival of apostolic doctrine that he sought—as opposed to the Gnostic heretical systems which he was combating. In the final paragraph of Book II he says:

Now, that the preaching of the apostles, the authoritative teaching of the Lord, the announcements of the prophets, the dictated utterances of the apostles, and the ministration of the law—all of which praise one and the same Being, the God and Father of all, and not many diverse beings, nor one deriving his substance from different gods or powers, but [declare] that all things [were formed] by one and the same Father (who nevertheless adapts [His works] to the natures and tendencies of the materials dealt with), things visible and invisible, and, in short, all things that have been made [were created] neither by angels, nor by any other power, but by God alone, the Father—are all in harmony with our statements, has, I think, been sufficiently proved, while by these weighty arguments it has been shown that there is but one God, the Maker of all things.

It is in the early chapters of Irenaeus' Book III that the Roman episcopal succession and pre-eminence has its strongest advocacy. (A careful translation of the Latin, however, removes the grounds of the present-day claim of Roman supremacy.) Here the author relates how the traditional doctrines of the orthodox church are more valid than the Gnostic claims because the former are more ancient—which causes him to enumerate a table of Roman bishops. In this context Irenaeus sets forth the church as the custodian of a certain true doctrine, to which he refers many times and depicts it in the familiar phrases (with some variation) of the Apostolic Confession.[14] His argument is contained in the caption of Chapter IV, "The Truth is to be Found Nowhere else but in the Catholic Church, the sole Depository of Apostolical Doctrine. Heresies are of Recent Formation, and Cannot Trace their Origin up to the Apostles." He says that there are churches not (yet) having the scriptures but which were reached by apostolic preaching and thus have the true faith. In our search for restoration ideas we are here back close to the fond preference of Papias for "the living and abiding voice." Restorationism is integral to this position, but not the more modern idea of a pattern church based upon scriptural blueprints or specifications. It is rather the Roman concept of an unbroken succession of tradition.

The concluding paragraphs of Chapter XIV in Book IV provide an excellent opportunity for presenting the New Testament church as in harmony with "the celestial patterns, and the spiritual images, and the types of things to come" which Irenaeus here discusses. This opportunity, however, is not employed. The typology section continues for quite a space beginning again at Chapter XX, and the claim of (plural) presbyterial succession to the apostles is seen in Chapter XXVI. Throughout, Irenaeus is concerned not about the reproduction of a scriptural pattern of the church but rather desires "to hold in suspicion others who depart from the primitive succession."[15] Instead of restoring a pattern church couched in apostolic scripture he pleads for obedience to presbyters in the church

---

[14]I surmise that it is precisely in this manner by repetitious use of a chosen line of doctrinal defenses (as a body of soldiers selects favorable terrain as its prime defense positions) around a favored body of beliefs, that the creedal process had the origin of its checkered career in Christianity. Time and again Irenaeus retreated to his chosen fortifications of doctrine. The habitual use of these phrases made them available for use when some body of resolutions or specifications of position seemed desirable. Mental habits are dominated by repetition. Irenaeus' recurring use of stock phrases in this voluminous writing may account for the dominance of creedal Christianity in ensuing centuries.

[15]Chapter XXVI.

who possess apostolic doctrine by means of their succession in office.[16]

VII

The assemblies of Christians in the middle of the second century were made up of people of the most modest attainments.

. . . After the manner of the synagogue, there came a moment when the "president" said, "Brethren, if ye have any word of exhortation for the people, say on." But the tongues were ceasing, as the apostle foretold; and they who professed to speak by the Spirit were beginning to be doubted. "Your fathers, where are they? and the prophets, do they live forever?" It was gratifying to the older men, and excited the curiosity of the young, when the reader stood up and said, "Hear, then, the word of Hermas."[17]

The Shepherd of Hermas enjoyed a rare popularity in the church of the second to fourth centuries. It took the form of a novel, with visions and movement and color. In Vision III, chapter 3, Hermas is shown a tower being built by six young men. Says the Lady:

. . . The tower which you see building is myself, the Church, who have appeared to you now and on the former occasion. Ask, then, whatever you like in regard to the tower, and I will reveal it to you, that you may rejoice with the saints.

The church is then set forth largely in terms of the Christian ethical virtues (the seven young women around the tower), with obvious comments upon the dangers of wealth. Book II, the Commandments, continues the instruction for personal living. The figure of the vine, which dominates Book III, Similitudes, leads in Similitude VIII, Chapter 6, to a reference to the church which seems aptly designed to teach something about its New Testament outline but turns out in the succeeding chapters to be a call to repentance for holy living.

---

[16]Chapter XXXII; also Preface to Book V.

[17]F. Crombie, M.A., "Introductory Note to the Pastor of Hermas," *Ante-Nicene Fathers*, Volume II, p. 6.

Similitude IX is about the building of the tower (the church) "according to his pleasure" (the Lord's). Again the consciousness of sins of the flesh dominates the narrative, and the stones are eventually[18] revealed to be certain personal virtues for living so as to glorify the church.[19]

VIII

There is no instruction for our purposes in Tatian's *Address to the Greeks* (written before A.D. 172). The rather extensive works of Theophilus of Antioch (before A.D. 181) are also barren of the type of interest which our subject involves.

IX

The extant writings of Clement of Alexandria occupy in one edition some 450 large, double-columned pages of small print. Apparently they were composed in the last quarter of the second century. His *Exhortation to the Heathen* exhibits a masterly knowledge of the poets, whom he uses to confute their pagan worship.

In *The Instructor* Clement begins to refer to the Church, "which is made perfect by her royal Head."[20] This is a good book in which to expect the setting forth of any singular plan for the church in its organization and life. Clement says:

. . . with the greatest clearness, accordingly, the Word has spoken respecting Himself by Hosea: "I am your Instructor." . . .

But our Instructor is the holy God Jesus, the Word, who is the guide of all humanity.[21]

The reading of Clement reminds one that he does not have to examine many books of the Ante-Nicene Fathers before he perceives that their interest is in a true Restorationism—of a type, or types. That is to say, they are concerned, as in the case of the eloquent and admirable Clement, to recapture the alto-

---

[18]Chapter XV.
[19]Chapter XVIII f.
[20]Chapter V.
[21]Chapter VII.

gether lovely and loving attitude toward men which he finds at its full beauty in Jesus. It is the Christ, the prophets, and the Psalmist who are repeatedly quoted by these disciples. Here are men enamored of the simplicities of faith and trust and love and righteous living which were characteristic of the spiritual guides just mentioned. Theirs are the attitudes and faiths Clement would restore. The Four Gospels, the Psalms, and the prophets are his principal sourcebooks.[22]

Perhaps there is such a thing, from a modern point of view, as carrying the restoration of a certain ethic or community-way-of-life too far. Note, for example, the chapter titles of *The Instructor,* Book II:

Chapter I	On Eating
Chapter II	On Drinking
Chapter III	On Costly Vessels
Chapter IV	How to Conduct Ourselves at Feasts
Chapter V	On Laughter
Chapter VI	On Filthy Speaking
Chapter VII	Directions for Those Who Live Together
Chapter VIII	On the Use of Ointments and Crowns
Chapter IX	On Sleep
Chapter X	Quaenam de Procreatione Liberorum Tractanda Sint
Chapter XI	On Clothes
Chapter XII	On Shoes
Chapter XIII	Against Excessive Fondness for Jewels and Gold Ornaments

There is some entertaining reading here, though not designed to be of this nature. Clement pours scorn on "gluttons, surrounded with the sound of hissing frying pans":

. . . Dishonouring the good and saving work of the Word, the consecrated *agape,* with pots and pouring of sauce; and by drink and delicacies and smoke desecrating that name, they are deceived in

---

[22] I counted all the Bible references in Book I of *The Instructor,* and found them to total 222; 145 of these were from the three sources mentioned: gospels 74, prophets 47, psalms 24.

their idea, having expected that the promise of God might be bought with suppers. Gathering for the sake of mirth, and such entertainments as are called by ourselves, we name rightly suppers, dinners, and banquets, after the example of the Lord.[23]

It will be noted that even the title of Chapter X is of too delicate a nature to be translated, as is the text of the chapter—and all of Book II of the *Stromata*. Clement overlooked nothing in his restoration program. Book III of his *Instructor* expands his account of how the Christian should dress, eat, etc.

After a wordy introduction to Book I of the *Stromata*, Clement outlines at the conclusion of Chapter I the items he intends to discuss. The idea of the nature of the church, and especially of a revealed pattern for it, is not in this summary, nor in the remainder of the work. The importance of the church's unity, however, is not absent from Clement's mind. He says:

. . . I do not think that philosophy directly declares the Word, although in many instances philosophy attempts and persuasively teaches us probable arguments; but it assails the sects. Accordingly it is added: "for he hath forsaken the ways of his own vineyard, and wandered in the tracks of his own husbandry." Such are the sects which deserted the primitive Church. Now he who has fallen into heresy passes through an arid wilderness, abandoning the only true God, destitute of God, seeking waterless water, reaching an uninhabited and thirsty land, collecting sterility with his hands. And those destitute of prudence, that is, those involved in heresies, "I enjoin," remarks Wisdom, saying, "Touch sweetly stolen bread and the sweet water of theft"; the Scripture manifestly applying the terms bread and water to nothing else but to those heresies, which employ bread and water in the oblation, not according to the canon of the Church.[24]

The church's unity is evidently at this early juncture calculated upon such items as the fellowship itself came to agree upon, and not upon a previously decreed New Testament organizational diagram. Such a diagram could most handily have been included in the range of topics which Clement brings forth

[23]Chapter I.
[24]Chapter XIX.

in Book V, beginning at Chapter VI, entitled "The Mystic Meaning of the Tabernacle and Its Furniture." But it is not there.

The ideal opportunity for Clement to present a New Testament diagram church is in Book VII, Chapter XV, entitled "The Objection to Join the Church on Account of the Diversity of Heresies Answered." In empire society there were many then, as there are today, who excused themselves from religious responsibility by saying that "the discord of the sects" must come to harmonious agreement before they would take membership and duties in the religious organization. Clement gives full and clear reply, noting that this problem of diversity is common in all areas of life, and that, for example, we do not refuse to philosophize because philosophers are not agreed, that we do not refrain from travel because some roads lead to a precipice, but rather in all things do we seek the true and safe course. "So also," he says, "are we bound in no way to transgress the canon of the Church." Chapter XVI is headed, "Scripture the Criterion by Which Truth and Heresy Are Distinguished."

Here we seem to reach the threshold of a present-day restoration ideology. Clement says, "Our Gnostic" [he had long labored to capture the term "Gnostic" as a proper title for the true Christian] "then alone, having grown old in the Scriptures, and maintaining apostolic and ecclesiastic orthodoxy in doctrine, lives most correctly in accordance with the Gospel, and discovers the proofs, for which he may have made search (sent forth as he is by the Lord) from the law and the prophets." This, of course, is not New Testament restorationism. Chapter XVII is entitled "The Tradition of the Church Prior to That of the Heresies." After establishing the chronological priority of the apostles and their teaching to the Gnostic heretics, he says:

From what has been said, then it is my opinion that the true Church, that which is really ancient, is one, and that in it those who according to God's purpose are just, are enrolled. For from the very reason that God is one, and the Lord one, that which is in the highest degree honourable is lauded in consequence of its singleness, being an imitation of the one first principle. In the nature of the One, then, it associated in a joint heritage the one Church which they strive to cut asunder into many sects.

Therefore in substance and idea, in origin, in pre-eminence, we say that the ancient and Catholic Church is alone, collecting as it does into the unity of the one faith—which results from the peculiar Testaments, or rather the one Testament in different times by the will of the one God, through one Lord—those already ordained, whom God predestinated, knowing before the foundation of the world that they would be righteous.

But the pre-eminence of the Church, as the principle of union, is, in its oneness, in this surpassing all things else, and having nothing like or equal to itself.

As the translator's brief footnote indicates, "This chapter illustrates what the Nicene Fathers understood by their language about the 'One, Holy, Catholic and Apostolic Church'." Clement's feeling toward the Gnostic heretics is caught in the title of Chapter XVIII, "The Distinction Between Clean and Unclean Animals in the Law Symbolical of the Distinction Between the Church, and Jews, and Heretics." The true burden of this section (Book VII ends at this point, and the theme changes) is perhaps epitomized by Henry Hart Milman, famous historian of Latin Christianity, who says of this time and condition:

All the churches of the West were Greek religious colonies. Their language was Greek, their organization Greek, their writers Greek, their Scriptures Greek; and many vestiges and traditions show that their ritual, their Liturgy was Greek. Through Greek the communication of the churches of Rome of the West was constantly kept up with the East. . . .

Thus the Roman church was but one of a confederation of Greek religious republics, founded by Christianity.[25]

This confederation was the Holy Catholic Church. It is true that as Clement says, the Scriptures were the final testing ground of its tradition. The sincere student of the great Greek-Christian philosopher will probably agree, however, that the

---

[25]From *History of Latin Christianity* (1903), p. 54.

restoration idea in the sense in which it has been cherished by modern restorers is absent from his mind and pages.[26] His constant emphasis is upon perception of true Christian philosophy or gnosis. Jerome proclaimed him the most learned of the ancients, which one may readily credit to be true when he reads Clement's manifold citations from the vast range of pagan authors. This learning Clement dedicated to the task which is indicated in the full title of the *Stromata:* "Titus Flavius Clement's Miscellaneous Collection of Speculative (Gnostic) Notes Bearing Upon the True Philosophy."

X

The seven hundred double-columned pages of Volume III in the printed edition of the Ante-Nicene Fathers used here do not suffice to include all of the extant writings of Tertullian (145-220). Chapter XXXIX of his *Apology* contains a description of Christian worship in his day. The account reminds us that if most modern advocates should succeed in their restoration program, they would have to revive the observance of the love feast of the New Testament Christians. Tertullian says:

. . . The Greeks call it *agape,* i.e., affection. Whatever it costs, our outlay in the name of piety is gain, since with the good things of the feast we benefit the needy; not as it is with you, do parasites aspire to the glory of satisfying their licentious propensities, selling themselves for a belly-feast to all disgraceful treatment,—but as it is with God himself, as a peculiar respect is shown to the lowly. If the object of our feast be good, in the light of that consider its further regulations. As it is an act of religious service, it permits no vileness or immodesty. The participants, before reclining, taste first of prayer to God. As much is eaten as satisfies the cravings of hunger; as much is drunk as befits the chaste. They say it is enough, as those who remember that even during the night they have to worship God; they talk as those who know that the Lord is one of their auditors. After manual ablution, and the bringing in of lights each is asked to stand forth and sing, as he can a hymn

---

[26]Among works of Clement which he refers to as written or about to be written (and which we long to have for a study of this kind) are *On the Unity and Excellence of the Church,* and *On the Office of Bishop, Presbyter, Deacons, and Widows.*

to God, either one from the holy Scriptures, or one of his own composing,—a proof of the measure of his drinking. As the feast commenced with prayer, so with prayer it is closed.

This may be as good a place as any to make an observation about the many restoration movements which have appeared in the course of the centuries, and that is that *each movement soon settled upon the particular things it preferred to restore.* We may develop this idea more fully elsewhere. Just here we notice that the *agape* was a New Testament practice. Few modern restorationists have made any perceptible effort to revive it. Current restorers are like a pacifist trying to establish his position on the authority of the 6th Commandment. "Thou shalt not kill" was not a universalism—as witnesses the fact that, on the day he brought the revelation of the Ten Commandments, Moses led in slaying 3,000 of his brethren. It simply meant "Don't kill anybody you shouldn't kill." Perhaps the modern restorers likewise have been trying to create universalism from particular observances and practices which grew out of the experience of a given day or generation. Like the pacifist faith, which must be founded on something more than a Siniatic authoritarianism, a valid restorationism must take its rise, and create its formal expressions, in the realm of New Testament attitudes, ways of life, and spiritual convictions. A single proof text is not enough.

The sort of Christianity Tertullian wanted to restore is not obscure in his writings. Defending his companions in the faith against the charge of being harm-doers in the empire,[27] he concludes with this bold tribute to commonly recognized Christian character:

. . . When Christians are brought before you on the mere ground of their name, is there ever found among them an ill-doer of the sort? It is always with your fold the prison is steaming, the mines are sighing, the wild beasts are fed: it is from you the exhibitors of gladiatorial shows always get their herds of criminals to feed

[27]*Apology*, Chapter XLII.

up for the occasion. You find no Christian there, except simply as being such; or if one is there as something else, a Christian he is no longer.[28]

"We, then, alone are without crime," he exults. Perhaps he was the latest of the Fathers who could make this claim (as he likewise seems to be the first to advise us that Christians had now begun to become soldiers).[29] What becomes plain is that his restoration program is for an ethic, a way of life. Chapter XLVI climaxes this plea. It appears numberless times. In *De Spectaculis* he says, "For what is our wish but the apostle's, to leave the world, and be taken up into the fellowship of our Lord?"[30]

Another observation is prompted by Tertullian's *On Idolatry*. The restoration principle in some modern expositions presupposes a static sort of diagrammed church, capable of being blueprinted, "once for all delivered to the saints." Certain authors, W. E. Garrison among them, have made it clear that restorationism's chief claim to unique service to the Christian world has been in calling attention to the New Testament soteriology, its terms of admission to the church and to salvation.[31] In Tertullian's writings a prime subject was: What occupations are un-Christian and make it impossible for their practicers to be admitted to the church? Chapter V and those following revolve around this problem. Tertullian definitely prescribes that idol makers "ought never to be admitted into the house of God." Yet in Chapter VII he acknowledges that some artificers have been advanced to the Christian ministry. Tertullian would not permit schoolmasters "nor all other professors of literature" to become Christians. This phase of the Christian conquest of ancient culture (or the ancient cultural conquest of Christianity) is a clear demonstration of the lack, at that time, of an apostolically diagramed ecclesiastical institution. Tertullian's appeal, indeed, in his handling of this problem, is to Moses, Joseph, Daniel, and other Old Testament worthies. He conceived

[28]Chapter XLIV.
[29]Chapter XLII.
[30]Chapter XXVIII.
[31]From *An American Religious Movement,* by W. E. Garrison, pp. 84, 85.

of the church as having the right, from biblical examples, in both the Old Testament and the New Testament, to rule upon new problems as they arose. It did not occur to him to suggest that the items of the plan of salvation had been apostolically fixed. Nor did he employ the way out of a problem such as the changing rightness of occupations in a changing social and moral order, as did Alexander Campbell in the slavery crisis when he said, "Slavery is a matter of opinion." The latter is a defensible attitude to take when a church with power in its forms rather than in its person-to-person relationships and with fixed items in its salvation *schema* is presupposed. Tertullian apparently did not entertain this presupposition. In *De Spectaculis* he dissociates himself from such literalism, saying:

. . . For the faith of some, either too simple or too scrupulous, demands direct authority from Scripture for giving up the shows, and holds out that the matter is a doubtful one, because such abstinence is not clearly in words imposed upon God's servants.[32]

In *De Corona* Tertullian presents a number of innovations in worship and ordinance forms, and says:

If, for these and other such rules, you insist upon having positive Scripture injunction, you will find none. Tradition will be held forth to you as the originator of them, custom as their strengthener, and faith as their observer. That reason will support tradition, and custom, and faith, you will either yourself perceive, or learn from someone who has. . . . The argument for Christian practices becomes all the stronger when also nature, which is the first rule of all, supports them.[33]

It is true that Tertullian refers to the apostles and their mode of life as the basis of his arguments, e.g., using their conduct as part of his argument in *De Corona* against wearing crowns. But, while he frequently presses home the force of this type of New Testament example, he never carries over the analogy to the matter of the structure and organization of the church. This is a significant omission.

---

[32]Chapter III.
[33]Chapters IV and V.

In Tertullian's *Prescription Against Heretics* we see the first near approach to a use of the ecclesiastical restoration idea. He says, "In the Lord's apostles we possess our authority; for even they did not of themselves choose to introduce anything, but faithfully delivered to the nations the doctrine [disciplinam] which they had received from Christ."[34] The reference is to the Gospel story proper, and not to an apostolically conceived church program, however, as we see in the next sentence: "If, therefore, even 'an angel from heaven should preach any other gospel,' he would be called accursed by us." The other portions of this chapter and context bear out our statement. The topics of the succeeding chapters are an almost perfect opportunity for introducing the idea of restoring the primitive, apostolic church, but it is not forthcoming. The doctrine to which reference was made soon is pointed up in Chapter XIII, where Tertullian gives his version of the Old Roman Symbol—the eventual Apostles' Creed. The chapter headings beginning at XX look definitely to be leading up to the restoration concept—only to end in the famous Tertullianic statement of apostolicity in terms of apostolic succession, where he says (in contradistinction to the usual and orthodox Roman Catholic lists) that Peter ordained Clement (rather than Linus and Cletus—Chapter XXXII).

"The statement of Augustine that before his death Tertullian returned to the bosom of the Catholic Church is very improbable," says David Schaff.[35] He "clung fast, in spite of his separation from the Catholic church, to his position that the church possesses the true doctrine, that the bishops *per successionem* are the repositories of the grace of the teaching office. . . ."[36] This is a very weak species of staff on which to lean in using the first patristic Latinist as a support for the modern Roman type of belief in apostolic succession, a practice they claim to have preserved or restored.

---

[34]Chapter VI.
[35]*The New Schaff-Herzog Encyclopedia of Religious Knowledge* (New York: Funk & Wagnalls, 1911), XI, p. 305.
[36]*Encyclopaedia Britannica* (Chicago: The Werner Co., 1893), XXIII, p. 197.

Again in Tertullian, as in Clement of Alexandria, we see the nature of the restorationism in which he was interested simply by noting the titles of some of his many writings. Separate books bear these superscriptions:

On the Apparel of Women
On the Veiling of Virgins
On Exhortation to Chastity
On Monogamy
On Modesty
On Fasting

In the first chapter of his *Veiling of Virgins* Tertullian again recapitulates the items of the incipient Apostles' Creed, which is called the "rule of faith," and adds, "This law of faith being constant, the other succeeding points of discipline and conversation admit the 'novelty' of correction." He then proceeds to "correct" the virgins about their dress. In all this we observe something quite different from an apostolic church pattern being restored; it is rather a new and human creedal church, plus "correction" of customs by arguments drawn from Scripture and other sources, including reason—and, of course, the episcopal organization.

The lack of any static or pattern concept of the church in Tertullian (apart from the "rule of faith" creedal definition) is evident in his Montanist epistle *To his Wife*. He says:

But although the Church did come in figuratively in the synagogue, yet (to interpret simply) it was necessary to institute (certain things) which should afterward deserve to be either lopped off or modified. . . . Therefore, by means of the wide licence of those days, materials for subsequent emendations were furnished beforehand, of which materials the Lord by his Gospel, and then the apostle in the last days of the (Jewish) age, either cut off the redundancies or regulated the disorders.[37]

A part of his argument or position (and against a static view of the discipline) is the next chapter heading, "Marriage Good: Celibacy Preferable."

[37]Chapter II.

49

XI

The *Octavius* of Minucius Felix need not detain us, since its content is much akin to that of Tertullian, and the principal argument of scholars familiar with the two authors is as to which is prior. The whole burden of the book is to present Christianity as a way of life superior to pagan manners.

XII

The Instructions of Commodianus in Favour of Christian Discipline Against the Gods of the Heathens (sic)—expressed in acrostics—would seem a likely place to set forth a true concept of the church. Such references to its nature as appear, however, make no use of the restoration concept or a specified apostolic diagram of it.

CHAPTER III

*The Restoration Concept
in the Ante-Nicene Fathers:
Origen to A.D. 325*

XIII

Origen (185-254), precocious and vastly learned, wrote prodigiously during his threescore and ten years. Typical of his encyclopedic products was his *Hexapla*, six-columned version of the Old Testament in fifty volumes. His works cover practically all areas of Christian thought.

In the preface to his *De Principiis* Origen seems about to bring us to the threshold of the ecclesiastical restoration principle for which we have looked in vain thus far in the Fathers. He says:

Seeing there are many who think they hold the opinions of Christ, and yet some of these think differently from their predeces-

51

sors, yet as the teaching of the Church, transmitted in orderly succession from the apostles, and remaining in the Churches to the present day, is still preserved, that alone is to be accepted as truth which differs in no respect from ecclesiastical and apostolical tradition.

Now it ought to be known that the holy apostles, in preaching the faith of Christ, delivered themselves with the utmost clearness on certain points which they believed to be necessary to every one, even to those who seemed somewhat dull in the investigation of divine knowledge. . . .

Once more, however, we find that the restoration of apostolic faith and life meant something quite different to this great man among the Fathers from what the principle means in modern restoration denominations. Origen immediately lists, in numbered paragraphs, precisely what he proposes in his program. Summarized, they are:

1. Correct theology
2. Correct Christology
4. Correct ideas about the human soul
3. Correct Pneumatology
5. Nonspeculation about pre-existence and the future
6. The essentially mysterious nature of the Scriptures

Origen does not fail to ascribe all necessary inspiration to the apostles for their special functions in the divine economy. In *De Principiis,* he says:

This being the state of the case, we shall sketch out, as if by way of illustration and pattern, what may occur to us with regard to the manner in which holy Scripture is to be understood on these several points, repeating in the first instance, and pointing out this fact, that the Holy Spirit, by the providence and will of God, through the power of His only-begotten Word, who was in the beginning God with God, enlightened the ministers of truth, the prophets and apostles, to understand the mysteries of those things or causes which take place among men, or with respect to men.[1]

---

[1]Book IV, Chapter I, paragraph 14.

He continues, immediately, however, to expound the theory of the nature of revelation for which he is so well known, i.e., that the true meaning of Old Testament scripture records is hidden and mysterious, "the history having taken place in appearance, and not literally." And, he quickly adds, "The Gospels themselves are filled with the same kind of narratives." Even if an outline of a primitive church were seen by Origen in the scriptures, we would not, according to him, expect the plain, surface description of this body to be the truth intended for revelation. As he says directly, "It was the design of the Holy Spirit, in those portions which appear to relate the history of events, rather to cover and conceal the meaning."[2]

In *Contra Celsus* Origen begins a defense of the apostles as good and inspired men.[3] The succeeding chapters portray their characters and functions. Here is a most available opportunity for setting forth their prerogatives as guardians and sponsors of a particular and unchanging church pattern—but the idea is not present in the pages. The same opportunity is most aptly present in Chapters XI ff. of Book III.

It is evident that difference of opinion about items of the Christian tradition early entered the church. It would be interesting to know just how much of Christian fellowship was extended to those mentioned by Origen in *Contra Celsus*.

Let no one, however, suspect that, in speaking as we do, we belong to those who are indeed called Christians, but who set aside the doctrine of the resurrection as it is taught in Scripture.[4]

Or, again:

. . . Let it be admitted, moreover, that there are some who accept Jesus, and who boast on that account of being Christians, and yet would regulate their lives, like the Jewish multitude, in accordance with the Jewish law—and these are the twofold sect of Ebionites, who either acknowledge with us that Jesus was born of a virgin, or deny this, and maintain that He was begotten like other human beings—what does that avail by way of charge

---

[2]*De Principiis*, Book IV, Chapter 23; *Contra Celsus*, Book IV, Chapter XLIX ff.
[3]Starting with Book I, Chapter LXII.
[4]Book V, Chapter XXII.

against such as belong to the Church, and whom Celsus has styled "those of the multitude"?[5]

The clue to an answer to our question is given soon:

. . . And if those who hold different opinions will not be convinced, we observe the injunction laid down for the treatment of such: "A man that is a heretic, after the first and second admonition, reject, knowing that he that is such is subverted, and sinneth, being condemned of himself." Moreover, we who know the maxim, "Blessed are the peacemakers," and this also, "Blessed are the meek," would not regard with hatred the corrupters of Christianity, nor term those who had fallen into error Circes and flattering deceivers.[6]

Origen, like other of the Fathers, longs to restore the ways and faith of Jesus—even in a war situation. Discussing such timely topics as: How to resist evil dictators, and What would happen if everybody in the State took the Christian (pacifist, as Origen defines it) stand, he says:

But if all the Romans, according to the supposition of Celsus, embrace the Christian faith, they will, when they pray, overcome their enemies; or rather, they will not war at all, being guarded by that divine power which promised to save five entire cities for the sake of fifty just persons. For men of God are assuredly the salt of the earth: they preserve the order of the world; and society is held together as long as the salt is uncorrupted: for "if the salt have lost its savour, it is neither fit for the land nor for the dunghill; but it shall be cast out, and trodden under foot of men. He that hath ears, let him hear" the meaning of these words. When God gives to the tempter permission to persecute us, then we suffer persecution; and when God wishes us to be free from suffering, even in the midst of a world that hates us, we enjoy a wonderful peace, trusting in the protection of Him who said, "Be of good cheer, I have overcome the world."[7]

Some later-discovered works of the voluminous Origen are published in Volume IX of the Fathers, and include his *Com-*

[5]Chapter LXI.
[6]Chapter LXIII.
[7]Book VIII, Chapter LXX.

mentary on John's Gospel. Employing his famous and brilliant—but unhistorical and outmoded—allegorical method of interpreting the scripture, the author has no real need, of course, for any specific description or plan of the church in his thought. It is Book I, Chapter XXIV in the *Commentary* before Origen mentions the church, and then in the following very significant attitude toward it:

. . . Thus we see the Church, the bride, to present an analogy to the moon and stars, and the disciples have a light, which is their own or borrowed from the true sun, so that they are able to illuminate those who have no command of any spring of light in themselves. We may say that Paul and Peter are the light of the world, and that those of their disciples who are enlightened themselves, but are not able to enlighten others, are the world of which the Apostles were the light. But the Saviour, being the light of the world, illuminates not bodies, but by His incorporeal power the intellect, to the end that each of us, enlightened as by the sun, may be able to discern the rest of the things of the mind. And as when the sun is shining the moon and the stars lose their power of giving light, so those who are irradiated by Christ and receive His beams have no need of the ministering apostles and prophets— we must have courage to declare this truth—nor of the angels; I will add that they have no need even of the greater powers when they are disciples of that first-born light.

Thus, far from being equal in inspiration and revelation, the apostles are lesser satellites of the central sun, Jesus, and enlightened Christians really have no need of their instruction. Indeed, even if Origen were to discover in the scriptures a pattern for the church, it would have little if any contribution to make to our subject, as witnesses the title of Book X, Chapter 4—"Scripture Contains Many Contradictions, and Many Statements Which Are Not Literally True, but Must Be Read Spiritually and Mystically." Succeeding chapters are an elaboration of this theme. Chapters 20, 23, and 26 refer to the church, but in figures and metaphors removed from practical significance.

It is Matthew only of the Gospel writers who uses the word "church" or makes direct reference to the institution. We move, therefore, with expectation to Origen's *Commentary* on this Gospel and especially to chapters 16 and 18 where the two uses of the word are found. On the Great Confession, Origen comments:

. . . And if we too have said like Peter, "Thou art the Christ, the Son of the living God," not as if flesh and blood had revealed it unto us, but by light from the Father in heaven having shone in our hearts, we become a Peter, and to us there might be said by the Word, "Thou art Peter," etc. For a rock is every disciple of Christ of whom those drank who drank of the spiritual rock which followed them, and upon every such rock is built every word of the church, and the polity in accordance with it; for in each of the perfect, who have the combination of words and deeds and thoughts which fill up the blessedness, is the church built by God.[8]

Succeeding paragraphs argue that not only Peter but also the other apostles share in the promise of binding and loosing. Further, instead of limiting promises and privileges to the apostolic circle, Origen in his "deeper and more spiritual" understanding of the scripture adds:

. . . *Many* then will say to the Saviour, "Thou art the Christ, the Son of the living God," but not all who say this will say it to Him, as not at all having learned it by the revelation of flesh and blood but by the Father in heaven Himself taking away the veil that lay upon their heart. . . . And if *any one* says this to Him not by flesh and blood revealing it until Him but through the Father in heaven, he will obtain the things that were spoken according to the letter of the Gospel to that Peter, but, as the spirit of the Gospel teaches, to every one who becomes such as that Peter was.[9]

Following chapters repeat and elucidate this inclusive promise—which, incidentally, places the great exegete in strict opposition to the Roman claim of Petrine supremacy. Chapter XVI repeats the argument once more. To fail to read the whole of this chapter would be to misunderstand the meaning of its

---

[8]Book XII, Chapter 10.
[9]Chapter 11, italics added.

concluding sentence (of which the final four words are determinative):

. . . According to this, then, through that which was said to the Apostles an outline was given beforehand of the teaching which would afterwards come to be of service both to them *and to every teacher*.

Origen's comments on the Matthew 18:17 reference to the church are entirely practical and contain no allusion to the subject of our inquiry.

XIV

There are a great number of instances, of course (Hippolytus, *Refutation,* Book XI, Chapter VII is only one example), where the Christian apologists refer to a Pauline or other New Testament admonition or church practice as justification for the continuation of the same doctrine or behavior. Such arguments from precedent or antiquity are just that, however, and nothing more. They are quite short of and apart from a thoroughgoing and clearly perceived *principle,* as we see the restoration program stated by modern reformers.

Hippolytus (c. 160-235) has a work of some 150 large, double-columned pages entitled *The Refutation of All Heresies,* which, among other things, gives an account of the doctrinal vagaries of the church. The translator says:

. . . These heresies, whether deducible from attempts to Christianize the philosophy of Paganism, or to interpret the Doctrines and Life of our Lord by the tenets of Gnosticism and Oriental speculation generally, or to create a compromise with the pretensions of Judaism—these heresies, amid all their complexity and diversity, St. Hippolytus reduces to one common ground of censure—antagonism to Holy Scripture.[10]

This purposeful use of scripture should give countless opportunities for the citing of doctrines, practices, or attitudes which, in the judgment of Hippolytus, should be restored to the

---

[10]J. H. MacMahon, M.A., "Introduction to The Refutation of All Heresies," *Ante-Nicene Fathers,* Volume V, p. 7.

apostolic manner of observance. In the first nine books he asserts that he has covered the field, "the tenets of both all the Greeks and barbarians," and in Book X he promises to tell "in conclusion to all, what the Doctrine of the Truth is." Beginning at Chapter XXVIII he gets down to the business of summarizing the truth, which turns out to be a complex theory of God's nature and creative processes. The restoration principle is absent in Hippolytus. He may not have anticipated any need for a long enduring church, for in a fragment from his scripture commentaries he says:

. . . For as a ship, sailing in the sea, leaves no traces of her way behind her, so neither does the Church, which is situate in the world as in a sea, leave her hope upon the earth, because she has her life reserved in heaven; and as she holds her way here only for a short time, it is not possible to trace out her course.[11]

Hippolytus' panegyric on the church in his *Treatise on Christ and Antichrist,* paragraph 59, shows a view of it devoid of restoration concepts.

XV

The church bulks large in the writing of Cyprian (c. 200-258). He is the ecclesiastical bedfellow of Ignatius, earliest advocate of *ecclesia in episcope* (not *in papa*) and the forerunner of Hincmar, Gerbert, and the modern Old Catholics. The church suffered the Decian persecution in Cyprian's day, and he became a martyr while Bishop of Carthage. For this and other reasons the church, its nature and function, is the subject of much of his writing.

Cyprian's first use of the restoration idea[12] has no reference to our theme but only to the need of the church being restored to good order following the hindrances of the great persecution.

Instead of the principle of ecclesiastical or organizational restoration operating in Cyprian we observe its opposite, the principle of development. Our pages would be expanded tre-

---

[11]On Proverbs, *Ante-Nicene Fathers,* V, p. 174.
[12]Epistle VII, paragraph 8.

mendously if we should merely summarize the new items of privilege which he defends for his clergy and which have no mention or suggestion in the truly primitive church.

Cyprian does refer to a danger of incurring "the Lord's displeasure" when presbyters "remembering neither the Gospel nor their own place . . . claim to themselves entire authority," (Epistle IX, 1); and he enjoins, in Epistle XV, 4, the observance of the "Lord's commands," and the "Gospel discipline"; but this is as near as he comes to suggesting that there was a fixed, apostolic or "gospel" pattern of the church organization which was to be followed in succeeding times. Rather does he take an attitude quite apart from the New Testament, as when he argues from "my episcopal authority". (IX, 2.)

Much reading of the Fathers brings one around to notice that such restoration of discipline, ethics, or other phases of Christian life as may be suggested, is derived from the Gospels and the examples of Jesus, much more than from the apostles. This is natural and to be expected, and is a different emphasis from the dominant interest of some modern restorationists in the apostles and an apostolic church. Indeed, we may say that while the apostles are highly and frequently honored in the Fathers, the order of interest in Christian leaders, on the part of these worthies and their fellow members was (1) Jesus, (2) recent martyrs, and (3) the apostles. Again, this is a natural psychology. Jesus was the founder and Savior, and recent martyrs were his best-known advocates. The apostles were of greater historic import—but teachers of church history are not likely to deceive themselves by thinking that most people are influenced (interested) more by weighty historic examples than by current or at least recent embodiments of principle. We may paraphrase a well-known saying and opine as follows: a martyr in the community is worth two apostles in antiquity. Choosing somewhat at random, we may cite Epistle XXIX as an example of this principle.

Epistle XXXIX, which relates the excommunication of Felicissimus and others, gives an excellent opportunity to present the church as an apostolically diagramed entity from which these men had strayed. Cyprian does not base his case on such an hypothesis, however (the apostles are not even mentioned in the many references to the church), but on his own conception of the universal episcopate.

In one respect Cyprian might well be named the Ante-Nicene patron saint of the restoration concept, for of all the Fathers he was the principal advocate of Christian unity. In Epistle XL he inveighs against those seeking "to distract the members of Christ into schismatical parties, and to cut and tear the body of the Catholic Church. . . ." He takes up the theme again in Epistle XLI, saying, "For this, my brother, we especially both labour after, and ought to labour after, to be careful to maintain as much as we can the unity delivered by the Lord, and through His apostles to us their successors. . . ." Several letters then follow, all dealing with the problem of unity in the light of a defection of some officers from the episcopal fellowship of that area. In all this correspondence there is no reference to an apostolic, scriptural standard of the church, but rather is "ecclesiastical discipline" (Epistle XLVIII, 2) the measuring rod of obedience. Of course, in his exposition of the Lord's Supper (Epistle LXII) the scripture precedents are employed—managing, however, to find justification for mixing water in the communion wine. Throughout, it is the dictate of the episcopate which in Cyprian is the determining counsel. We look in vain through these numerous and lengthy epistles for the concept of a perfect, patterned church preached by the apostles. Such hints as there are in the direction of the ecclesiastical restoration concept arise principally in Cyprian's controversies, especially his contest with Stephen, Bishop of Rome, on baptism. Cyprian says:

. . . But we join custom to truth, and to the Romans' custom we oppose custom, but the custom of truth; holding from the beginning that which was delivered by Christ and the apostles.[13]

How familiar this sounds! I have the truth from the apostles—you have only a custom.

[13]LXXIV, 19.

Cyprian is best remembered for his Treatise on the Unity of the Church because it deals with the way the organization should be ruled. Interpolations were added to the text by later writers in order to aid the cause of universal rule by the Roman bishop. What must inescapably strike our attention in a study of this kind is the absence of any suggestion that the unity of the church may be realized by restoring an apostolic pattern of it. Such an idea is nowhere present in this key work of the Fathers in the field of our investigation. What looks like the beginning of such a concept is introduced in paragraph 25, but promptly turns out to be another matter.

The remaining epistles of Cyprian show the interests common to his day, and include exhortations to women to dress modestly, and to keep silent in the church. There is also much of ethical and devotional instruction, encouragement to martyrs, and other homilies.

XVI

Novatian (210-280) was a claimant to the title of Bishop of Rome. Like Tertullian, he was a puritan in his organizational interest, and thus was a true restorationist—i.e., the restorer of a certain quality and order of primitive Christian life. Such of his own writings as we have, however, are of a distinctly theological character *(On the Trinity, On Jewish Meats),* and contain no discussion about the church.

XVII

Gregory, called Thaumaturgus, the "wonder-worker" (c. 205-270), studied under Origen and became a bishop by stealth and absentee consecration when he hesitated to assume the responsibility of the office. He wrote on many subjects, his extant remains constituting some seventy large pages in the Ante-Nicene Fathers. His *Declaration of Faith,* like the historic ancient creeds, revolves around the Trinity and contains no reference to the church.

His *Canons* present an ideal opportunity for suggesting ideas about the nature of the church. It is taken up, however, with concern for the pressing problem of how to discipline members who had fallen away from the church under the ravages of the Goths in the days of Gallianus (259-267). Its interest is in a true restorationism—but of the kind useful in that day, a life restored to the primitive Christian way of daily behavior. The presumably spurious Canon Eleven concludes the treatise, saying, "Restoration is that one be associated with the faithful, and go not forth with the catechumens: and last of all comes the participation in the holy ordinances." These are steps three and four in a program for the return of lapsed members.

A Trinitarian and Christological interest dominates the *Sectional Confession of Faith* of twenty-three paragraphs attributed to Gregory. No thought of the church occurred to the author, as far as the evidence goes. The same thing is true of the *Twelve Topics of Faith*.

XVIII

The Dionysian controversy, between bishops of this same name at Rome and Alexandria, gave the resident of the latter see much occasion to discuss the person of Christ. This subject might readily have included such a topic as our Lord's continuing rule in the church, through scripture patterns or otherwise. Some might say that the mind of the great Alexandrian was above any form of literalism and cite his broad attitudes toward the scriptures as seen in his Epistle to Bishop Basilides, Canon I, discussing the hour of the closing of the fast of Pentecost.

In one of his extant fragments dealing with the millennial reign of Christ he indicates that "Some before our time have set aside his book" (Revelation). "Nay, further, they hold that it can be no sort of revelation because it is covered with so gross and dense a veil of ignorance." This, today, may seem a strange attitude to take to what is now a canonical book, but Dionysius' reason for accepting it is yet stranger. He says:

. . . I regard it as containing a kind of hidden and wonderful intelligence on the several subjects which come under it. For though I cannot comprehend it, I still suspect that there is some deeper sense underlying the words. And I do not measure and judge its expressions by the standard of my own reason, but, making more allowance for faith, I have simply regarded them as too lofty for my comprehension; and I do not fortwith reject what I do not understand, but I am only the more filled with wonder at it, in that I have not been able to discern its import.[14]

Any advocacy of a New Testament church based upon such an attitude toward the New Testament itself would hardly have much value. However, we are saved any embarrassment in this matter, for Dionysius' writings contain no ecclesiological reference. The only restoration philosophy observable in Dionysius is the ethical, way-of-life Christianity in which he praises the martyrs of his acquaintance. Concerning Nemesion, an Egyptian, burned between two robbers, he says, "Thus the blessed martyr was honoured after the pattern of Christ."[15]

XIX

Archelaus, the seat of whose bishopric is undetermined, engaged about the year 262 in an extensive disputation with Manes, author of the Manichaean heresy that was so long to disturb the peace of the church. While cosmological matters and the problems of good and evil dominate the discussion, the subject of our interest in this study has an appearance in paragraph 51 of the *Disputation*. Defending his ideas against the innovations of Manes, Archelaus says:

. . . From the loving desire for the Savior we have been called Christians, as the whole world itself attests, and as the apostles also plainly declare. Yea, further, that best master-builder of His, Paul himself, has laid our foundation, that is, the foundation of the Church, and has put us in trust of the law, ordaining ministers, and presbyters, and bishops in the same, and describing in the places severally assigned to that purpose, in what manner and with what character the ministers of God ought to conduct themselves, of what repute the presbyters ought to be possessed, and how they should be constituted, and what manner of persons those also ought to be who desire the office of bishop. And all these in-

[14]Extant Fragments, Part I, 1, 3.
[15]*Ibid.*, Part II, Epistle III, 7.

stitutions, which were once settled well and rightly for us, preserve their proper standing and order with us to this day, and the regular administration of these rules abides amongst us still.

Here, especially in the last sentence, is the first appearance in the Ante-Nicene Fathers of the ground of the idea that the Pauline scriptures are determinative in church organization. This is the ecclesiastical type of restorationism which has loomed so large in the plea of certain modern religious groups that propose to re-establish the church on primitive patterns.

XX

Alexander, bishop of Lycopolis in 301, writes in the first chapter of his treatise, *Of the Manichaeans,* on the origin of heresies among Christians. They come, he says, from those "sagacious in handling nice and subtle questions." Many "wish to become the heads of sects," he adds, and "there being no rule nor law by which a solution may be obtained of the things which are called in question, but, as in other matters, this ambitious rivalry running out into excess, there is nothing to which it does not cause damage and injury."

As one might expect from the writer of these lines, there is no conception in his mind of a church pattern once for all delivered to the saints. He says, concerning Jesus:

. . . in order that husbandmen, carpenters, builders, and other artisans, might not be driven away from good, He convened a common council of them altogether, and by simple and easy conversations He both raised them to a sense of God, and brought them to desire what was good.[16]

XXI

Restoration polity has usually been of congregational order, seeing the New Testament precedents for government in the forms favored by the anabaptist and independent groups rather than the more typically high Protestant programs of oligarchical government preferred by Luther and Calvin. It is not only of

[16]Chapter XVI.

some importance to note in the Fathers such instances of restoration ideology as may be ferreted out, but it is of equal significance to observe the lack of characteristically congregational ideals and the presence of concepts basically at variance with such a program. An instance of the latter is to be seen in the martyr Peter, bishop of Alexandria (d. 311), who is said by his biographer Anastasius to have "attained to the pontificate" (as the Alexandrian archbishopric then was termed), and who did not hesitate to name two priests who should "rule my church" after his decease.[17]

<h1 style="text-align:center">XXII</h1>

Methodius (260-312) served as bishop in various stations and was martyred in the last of the great persecutions of the church. His only complete extant work is the *Banquet of Ten Virgins*. Here is high praise of the virginal life, and Methodius causes Mercella to say of Jesus, "He, being God, was pleased to put on human flesh, so that we, beholding as on a tablet the divine Pattern of our life, should also be able to imitate Him who painted it."[18] The *Banquet* is another of the many Ante-Nicene works that seek to restore in the church community a certain type of primitive Christian behavior.

Discourse III, "Thaleia," employs much discussion of the church, but the principal ideas concerning it for which we have been seeking are not found there. Rather, instead of the church being revealed in pattern to the apostles, Discourse V, "Thallousa," Chapters VII and VIII, understands it to have been predetermined and forecast in the tabernacle of Old Testament times. The same idea is presented in Discourse IX, "Tusiane," Chapter II.

<h1 style="text-align:center">XXIII</h1>

The rhetorical and eloquent Lactantius (c. 250-325) outstripped the fame of his teacher, Arnobius, and was invited by the Emperor Diocletian to practice the art of philosophy at

---

[17]*The Genuine Acts of Peter.*
[18]Discourse I, Chapter IV.

65

Nicomedia. Settling in Gaul, to him was entrusted the education of the Emperor Constantine's son, Crispus. To the former, Lactantius addressed *The Divine Institutes,* a work in seven books, embracing more than 250 large, double-columned pages of print. The beautiful eloquence of this "Christian Cicero," a late-in-life convert to his new faith, here finds a subject and a master worthy of so fine a gift.

The parade of learning which Lactantius dedicates to the Christian faith moves in grandeur through half of its contents before coming to a consideration of any phase of the theme of our inquiry. The concluding chapter (XXX) of Book IV is entitled "Of Avoiding Heresies and Superstitions, and What Is the Only True Catholic Church." Heresy is traced to those who, "aiming at the increase of their wealth and honour, aspired to the highest sacerdotal power"—i.e., wrong polity or ecclesiastical disobedience and resulting rationalization of disputed doctrines. (Novatians, Marcionites, Arians and others are named.) Other than this, Lactantius' definition of the Catholic Church is simple:

. . . The true Catholic Church is that in which there is confession and repentence, which treats in a wholesome manner the sins and wounds to which the weakness of the flesh is liable.

Here, again, in the spirit of James is a definition of the Christian religion in terms of a type of life that the primitive church produced and which must be restored if the divine institution is to embody the purpose of its Founder.

XXIV

Victorinus, bishop of Pettau, in Austria, was martyred in 304. His Commentary on the Apocalypse of the Blessed John quite naturally includes many references to the church. We look in vain, however, for any designation of an apostolic pattern of this institution. The concluding paragraph, referring to Chapter 22 of the Apocalypse, gives the nearest approach to our theme:

. . . But the twelve gates we believe to be the number of the apostles, who, shining in the four virtues as precious stones, manifesting the light of their doctrine among the saints, cause it to enter the celestial city, that by intercourse with them the choir of angels may be gladdened. And that the gates cannot be shut, it is evidently shown that the doctrine of the apostles can be separated from rectitude by no tempest of contradiction. Even though the floods of the nations and the vain superstitions of heretics should revolt against their true faith, they are overcome, and shall be dissolved as the foam, because Christ is the Rock by which, and on which, the Church is founded.

XXV

The romance of the discovery of the *Teaching of the Twelve Apostles* at Constantinople in 1873 is an oft-told tale among students of early Christian writings, and an earnest, we may hope, of fascinating manuscripts yet to be recovered. The work apparently comes from a period within a century of the church's founding, as evidenced by "its simplicity, almost amounting to childishness," as M. B. Riddle says.

In connection with our study it is interesting to see that the *Teaching* reflects that early age of the church when there were many apostles, and not just "the twelve" of whom modern Christians usually think when contemplating an assumed model "apostolic church." Chapter XI says:

. . . Let every apostle that cometh to you be received as the Lord. But he shall not remain except one day; but if there be need, also the next; but if he remains three days, he is a false prophet. And when the Apostle goeth away, let him take nothing but bread until he lodgeth; but if he ask money, he is a false prophet.

Here as elsewhere there is evident a willingness on the part of the church to experiment in making regulations for dealing with apostles and others in their relations with the developing congregations. The opening chapters are in the spirit and much in the very wording of the Sermon on the Blessed Life. This is further substantiation of the conviction that grows upon a reader of the Fathers, that is, that the restoration in which they were interested was the reproduction of a daily behavior in life characteristic of the primitive Christian societies. For example, hear Chapter III, Verses 7-10:

. . . But be thou meek, since the meek shall inherit the earth. Be long-suffering and pitiful and guileless and gentle and good and always trembling at the words which thou hast heard. Thou shalt not exalt thyself, nor give overconfidence to thy soul. Thy soul shall not be joined with lofty ones, but with just and lowly ones shall it have its intercourse. The workings that befall these receive as good, knowing that apart from God nothing cometh to pass.

The brief Chapter XV gives two sentences to an admonition to appoint bishops and deacons, in typical New Testament phraseology. The concluding Chapter XVI shows plainly the expectation of the impending second coming of Jesus.

XXVI

The *Apostolic Constitutions* had as their purpose, say the editors, "to confirm the episcopal hierarchy, and to establish the unity of the Catholic church on the basis of the unity of the priesthood." But, "It is now generally held," said Professor Riddle (1886), "that the purpose of the compilation was merely to present a manual of instruction, worship, polity, and usage for both clergy and laity." Such a design, of course, should present us with precisely the ideas for which we are seeking— provided, of course, that these ideas were in the mind of the writer of the *Constitutions*.

The ethical idealism of apostolic days is emphasized throughout Book I of this work, entitled "Concerning the Laity." The same note is constant in Book II, describing the duties and character of Bishops, Presbyters, and Deacons. Typical is a sentence in Section IV: "As, therefore, you are patterns for others, so have you Christ for your pattern."

Instead of an apostolically conceived precedent for church organization the frequent appeal of the author of the *Constitu-*

tions is to the Old Testament patterns. As the growing episcopacy in church leadership was here enlarging its claims, the Old Testament monarchical forms were more suitable to the aspiring clergy than were the democratic equalities of the New Testament. This is apparent in Chapter XXX of Book II, quoted here in its entirety.

For now the deacon is to you Aaron, and the bishop Moses. If, therefore, Moses was called a god by the Lord, let the bishop be honored among you as a god, and the deacon as his prophet. For as Christ does nothing without His Father, so neither does the deacon do anything without his bishop; and as the Son without His Father is nothing, so is the deacon nothing without his bishop; and as the Son is subject to His Father so is every deacon subject to his bishop; and as the Son is the messenger and prophet of the Father, so is the deacon the messenger and prophet of his bishop. Wherefore let all things that he is to do with any one be made known to the bishop, and be finally ordered by him.

Of great interest is Book II, Section VII, "On Assembling in the Church," especially Chapter LVII, with its detailed description of how a church service should be arranged and conducted. The appeal to authority for these directions is not to the apostles or to any New Testament regulation. Instead, in the center of the chapter is this statement: "For the same description and pattern was both in the tabernacle of the testimony and in the temple of God."

Book VI, Chapter XII, purports to be a personal account by Peter of how the eleven apostles and other recognized leaders of the early church preached and defined Christian faith and church organization. It is principally a recounting of the Acts 9-15 record, and reflects the primacy of this group in determining all phases of church life.

XXVII

We have refrained from mention of many works in the Fathers wherein no comment is made upon the subject of our investigation. It would become monotonous to demonstrate the numerous instances in which a writer expounded his religious system, showing the providences of God and his provisions for the organization and promotion of the faith. Time and time again the Old Testament accounts of progress toward Christ are narrated, and a perfect setting is provided for the presentation of the church as the successor to the community of Israel and conveyor of the message of salvation. Time and again we are left mentally hanging loose in the process of history. Instead of a vision for the ages, and a church program fitted (in unchangeable norms) for millenniums to come, it is present ethical and pious living in anticipation of a consummation of the age, through Christ's coming again to earth, that concludes the presentation. For example, note this sequence of chapter titles in Book I of the Clementine Recognitions:

Chapter XXVII	Account of the Creation
Chapter XXVIII	Account of the Creation—Continued
Chapter XXIX	The Giants: the Flood
Chapter XXX	Noah's Sons
Chapter XXXI	World After the Flood
Chapter XXXII	Abraham
Chapter XXXIII	Abraham: His Posterity
Chapter XXXIV	The Israelites in Egypt
Chapter XXXV	The Exodus
Chapter XXXVI	Allowance of Sacrifice for a Time
Chapter XXXVII	The Holy Place
Chapter XXXVIII	Sins of the Israelites
Chapter XXXIX	Baptism Instituted in Place of Sacrifice
Chapter XL	Advent of the True Prophet
Chapter XLI	Rejection of the True Prophet
Chapter XLII	Call of the Gentiles
Chapter XLIII	Success of the Gospel
Chapter XLIV	Challenge by Caiaphas
. . .	
Chapter XLIX	Two Comings of Christ

70

In part, the last-named chapter reads:

. . . His coming, therefore, was predicted by Moses, who delivered the law of God to men; but by another also before him, as I have already informed you. He therefore intimated that He should come, humble indeed in His first coming, but glorious in His second. And the first, indeed, has been already accomplished; since He has come and taught, and He, the Judge of all, has been judged and slain. But at His second coming He shall come to judge, and shall indeed condemn the wicked, but shall take the pious into a share and association with Himself in His kingdom.

Book III of the same work purports to continue the words of Peter, and Chapter LXVI sees Zacchaeus made Bishop of Caesarea, enjoining the people as follows:

. . . You ought therefore to honour him as holding the place of Christ, obeying him for your salvation, and knowing that whatever honour and whatever injury is done to him, redounds to Christ, and from Christ to God. Hear him therefore with all attention, and receive from him the doctrine of the faith; and from the presbyters the monitions of life; and from the deacons the order of discipline. Have a religious care of widows, vigorously assist orphans; take pity on the poor; teach the young modesty; —and in a word, sustain one another as circumstances shall demand; worship God, who created heaven and earth; believe in Christ; love one another; be compassionate to all; and fulfill charity not only in word, but in act and deed.

In the *Homilies,* beginning with a reputed epistle of Clement to James, the church is referred to in episcopal terms. Peter is "the most sure foundation of the Church"[19] and persuades Clement to succeed him as bishop because he (Clement) "has learned better the regulations of the church"[20] and "because you have learned from me the administration of the church."[21]

The *Homilies* proper carry much reputed conversation between Peter and Clement. Peter quotes "scriptural" teachings of Jesus (II, LI, etc.) from an apocryphal source, and argues

[19]Chapter I.
[20]Chapter II.
[21]Chapter IV.

71

that there are "false scriptures," written "at the demand of evil" (III, V). Truth is "reserved for the grateful" (III, X) and not granted to all Christians. There is no ground here for any scriptural norm of a church.[22] Homily III, Chapter LX and following, states the theory of the "chair of Christ" handed on through Peter.

XXVIII

The Apocrypha of the New Testament, contained with the Ante-Nicene Fathers, is of very uneven quality. It is derived from a long-time range—some portions, by good authority, appearing in the first century, much of it before Nicea, but some rising as late as the Middle Ages.

The apocryphal material is divided into (1) Gospels, (2) Acts, and (3) Apocalypses. Remembering that the canonical Gospels mention the church only twice, we are not surprised that the theme of this investigation is absent from the pages of "gospel" material purporting to come from comparable antiquity. The Acts records are scarcely any more helpful. They reek with miracles. At the close of the *Acts of Andrew and Matthias,* "in the city of the man-eaters," we read:

. . . And after these things he drew a plan of a church, and he caused the church to be built. And he baptized them, and gave them the ordinances of our Lord Jesus Christ, saying to them: stand by these in order that ye may know the mysteries of our Lord Jesus Christ.

XXIX

The "Memoirs of Edessa and Other Syriac Documents" in Volume VIII of the Fathers are estimated by the editors to be "interesting relics of the primitive ages, but neither wholly gen-

---

[22]For a scholarly justification of this contention, see "The First Christian Novel; a Review of the Pseudo-Clementina," by John Lowe (*The Canadian Journal of Religious Thought,* September-October, 1931). Not only is the concept of apostolic authority for the norms or structure of the church absent in the Clementina, but a definitely anti-Pauline bias is clearly distinguishable in it. Says Lowe, "It looks as if certain Jewish circles had already in pre-Christian times become infiltrated with gnostic ideas and that 'baptist' sects representing such a fusion were serious rivals to the primitive Church" (p. 301). The article includes careful review of two detailed studies of the Literature: Carl Schmidt, *Studien zu den Pseudo-Clementinen* (Leipzig: J. C. Hinrichs, 1929); Oscar Cullman, *Le Problème Littéraire et Historique du Roman Pseudo-Clementin* (Paris: Alcan, 1930).

uine nor in details authentic." Eusebius in his fourth-century *Church History* included reference to some of this material, but Lardner thinks that it was of a date almost as late as that historian himself.

One of the ancient Syriac documents is entitled *The Teaching of the Apostles*. It purports to give details about the experience of the Day of Pentecost and its miracles. It says, "By the same gift of the Spirit which was given to them on that day, they appointed Ordinances and Laws," and enumerates them carefully as follows (abbreviated here):

1. Pray toward the east.
2. Let there be service on the first day of the week.
3. Let there be service on the fourth day of the week.
4. Let there be service on the eve of the Sabbath, 9th hour.
5. Elders, deacons, subdeacons, and an overseer.
6. Celebrate the day of Epiphany.
7. Observe a fast 40 days before the passion date; celebrate passion and resurrection.
8. People stand when Gospel is read.
9. Commemorate the Ascension.
10. Only Old Testament, and Prophets, Gospels and Acts to be read from the pulpit.
11-15. Rules for life of ministers.
16-27. Other regulations of life and worship.

They are followed by this interesting paragraph:

. . . All these things did the apostles appoint, not for themselves, but for those who should come after them—for they were apprehensive that in time to come wolves would put on sheep's clothing: since for themselves the Spirit, the Paraclete, which was in them, was sufficient that, even as He had appointed these laws by their hands, so He would guide them lawfully. For they, who had received from our Lord power and authority, had no need that laws should be appointed for them by others. For Paul also, and Timothy, while they were going from place to place, in the country of Syria and Cilicia, committed these same Commands and Laws of the apostles and elders to those who were under the hand of the apostles, for the churches of the countries in which they were preaching and publishing the Gospel.

It is further added:

. . . And after the death of the apostles there were Guides and Rulers in the churches; and, whatsoever the apostles had committed to them and they had received from them, they continued to teach to the multitude through the whole space of their lives. They, too again, at their deaths committed and delivered from the apostles; also what James had written from Jerusalem, and Simon from the city of Rome, and John from Ephesus, and Mark from Alexandria the Great, and Andrew from Phrygia, and Luke from Macedonia, and Judas Thomas from India: that the epistles of an apostle might be received and read in the churches that were in every place, just as the achievements of their Acts, which Luke wrote, are read; that hereby the apostles might be known, and the prophets and the Old Testament and the New; that so might be seen one truth was proclaimed in them all: that one Spirit spake in them all, from one God whom they had all worshipped and had all preached.

Integral to the traditions here related is that Syria received its preaching from "Addaeus the apostle, one of the seventy-two apostles" (the Syriac document, "Moses of Chorene," Chapter VIII, speaks of seventy-six apostles). This document is of a piece with others which profess to give details of how Peter preceded Paul to Rome and enjoyed "the rank of the Superintendence of Rulers twenty-five years." As the editors[23] of them say, "The chronological incredibility of this residence in Rome has been fully demonstrated . . . it is so entirely inconsistent with the scriptural history." This is scarcely safe ground for the drawing forth of reliable data about the preaching of the apostles, and what is enumerated above does not have the ring of scriptural precedent or authenticity about it.

[23]Alexander Roberts and James Donaldson, editors of the Edinburgh edition, *The Ante-Nicene Fathers* (Buffalo: Authorized American edition, The Christian Literature Co., 1886.

XXX

The fascinating story of the recovery of the text of the *Apology of Aristides* will not be retold here. Suffice it to say that this document preceded and set the pattern for Justin Martyr's *Apology,* usually thought of as the earliest of the major documents of the Fathers, and is presented late in the printed editions of these works only because of its late discovery and publication. It was originally presented to the Emperor Hadrian upon his visit to Athens in A.D. 125, says Eusebius, and the latest date proposed for it is during the reign of Antonius Pius (138-161).

The church receives no mention in this work. Instead here we see again the principal characteristic of early writings of the Fathers, the desire to portray and to induce benevolent, ethical ways of life that in their sight distinguished the Christian faith from other religions. Original Christianity was simple and yet truly distinguished as compared with its competitors. Organization, dogma, and fixed ritual receive not so much as a brief exposition here. Christianity to the early disciples was a new kind of practical life. This was its solvent for personal and social ills.

XXXI

Volume X of *Ante-Nicene Fathers* includes an extensive index to the contents of its nine predecessors. It seems significant that in the index there is no reference to the ideas we have sought in this examination, with the single exception of "Church: her officers appointed by the apostles," commented upon in the dubious material of Section XXIX of this chapter, on the Syriac documents.

Chapter IV

The Restoration Concept in the Ante-Nicene Fathers: Summary and Authorities

XXXII

What, then, was the restoration concept in the Ante-Nicene Fathers? We may summarize the preceding findings briefly.

Clement of Rome called for a restoration of the ethical "practice of peace" and benevolent living which was the primary need of the church in his day. *Ignatius* desired a species of mystical restorationism in which sufferings would lead to identity with the crucified Savior. *Papias* yearned for the reproduction of a Christian life in which books and legalisms should be subordinated to the "living and abiding voice" and the spiritual exaltation that could accompany it. *Justin Martyr* also pleaded for the revival of the ethical virtues of the Founder—as did *Barnabas*. *Irenaeus* shifted the ground of the discussion by pre-

76

scribing obedience to presbyters who possess correct doctrine by means of succession to apostolic offices.

Clement of Alexandria, with his "Gnostic notes on the True Philosophy" endeavored to outline in detail the behavior of Christians in all circumstances of life. Apostolic correctness needed the later "ecclesiastical orthodoxy in doctrine" to complete itself, in his view. The lack of an apostolically diagramed church order is attested in the time of *Tertullian* by his failure to use such an idea just when it would have proved most valuable. Indeed, he regarded lightly "the faith of some, either too simple or too scrupulous (which) demands direct authority from Scripture," to use his own words.

Origen, famous allegorizer of the scriptures, conceived them to be something quite different from the clear, understandable record that they must be to fulfill a patterned program of ecclesiastical restoration. He felt little dependence upon apostolic guidance, but believed that he and other leaders were "irradiated by Christ."

Hippolytus held the scriptures in highest regard because they provided him with a base from which to attack the heresies and religious competitors of Christianity. As to the church, however, it is as a ship on the sea and leaves no mark by which it can be traced. His interests were principally otherworldly, so he needed no long-continuing church on earth.

Development, not restoration, was the theme of *Cyprian,* who preferred what he termed "my episcopal authority" rather than scripture as his justification. *Novatian,* like others before and after him, wanted to feature the practical good life as the mark of the church. The same interest was primary in *Gregory Thaumaturgus,* and in *Dionysius of Alexandria,* whose ideas concerning parts of the New Testament leave no room for a scriptural restorationism.

Archelaus is the one Father of the Ante-Nicene period in whom we may find an expression of the restoration plea very much in the terms and ideology of the program of various modern Christian groups. The object of his specific reference is limited, however, to the scriptures produced by the apostle Paul.

Alexander of Lycopolis has no contribution to our theme. The martyr *Peter* was of the opinion expressed by Cyprian in preferring episcopal authoritarianism. *Methodius* re-echoes the most frequent type of restoration idealism in the Fathers—the desire for a reproduction of a superior moral life as the distinctive work of the church. To this opinion inclines also the eloquent *Lactantius*.

Victorinus does not touch upon our theme. The anonymous *Teaching of the Twelve Apostles* reflects from its very early date of origin the ethical idealism of the Sermon on the Blessed Life. The same note appears frequently in the earlier portions of the *Apostolic Constitutions,* but later the idea of episcopal authority is dominant in its thought of the church, based upon Old Testament precedents. The *Clementine* literature, of questionable value, shares the latter view. There is nothing to help our study in the *Apocrypha of the New Testament.*

There is a pseudepigraphical ring that characterizes the *Memoirs of Edessa and Other Syriac Documents,* but like such materials they are exceedingly interesting. Plenty of ecclesiastical restorationism (as we have preferred to term the formal, normative, or institutional ideal) is present in this literature, but not of a kind that would help a historically intelligent restoration movement, because of the irrelevance of the observances that are featured therein.

To conclude with a characteristic note, the Apology of *Aristides* would restore to the church those benevolent, ethical ways of life which the example of Jesus gave it as a birthright. In brief, if the whole range of Christian life be included under the heads of ethical, mystical, theological, and institutional experiences, the desire of the Ante-Nicene Fathers was to restore to the church these elements, and in this order.

XXXIII

The findings in the foregoing examination of the works of the apostolic and Ante-Nicene Fathers of the church may be verified in a host of eminent authorities. So far as we know, none of them has taken occasion to trace out the specific ideas for which we have been searching. Apparently they have not felt that such conceptions are of lively importance for the Christian community today. If the pattern of an ideal church organization were in the mind of the apostles and fathers, the leading students of their literary remains would be expected to notice the existence and weigh the importance of such a theme. Let us see what a few representative scholars have to say on the subject.

(1)

The old but still standard work of Edwin Hatch, *The Organization of the Early Christian Churches* constituting the Bampton Lectures for 1880, embraces the patristic sources in discussing primitive Christian organization. Pointing out the apostolic direction of the process by which structure was achieved in the church, Hatch shows that it was growth or change in apostolic intention which brought new forms of organization and episcopal determination of doctrine in individual churches where apostles had labored. That the apostles had handed to the local leaders (changed by social needs to a single leader, as Jerome affirms) a specific pattern of church organization is denied. He says, "There is no proof that the words of Holy Scripture in which the unity of the Church is expressed or implied refer exclusively, or at all, to unity of organization."[1] Rather was the earliest "basis of Christian fellowship . . . a changed life."[2] Persons who cannot rest content until they have forced identity of formal structure and ritual upon their brethren may see their logical ancestors in certain ancient advocates of the "iron bedstead" idea of ecclesiastical measurement whose efforts resulted in time in the Roman centralization.

The concluding pages of this seasoned work are worthy of careful study. Hatch says:

On the hypothesis that the constitution of the Christian societies was settled by the Apostles in their lifetime, and that what

---

[1]From *The Organization of the Early Christian Churches,* by Edwin Hatch, p. 186. Copyright 1895 by Longmans, Green & Co., Inc. Some of Hatch's work is now being republished in the Harper Torchbook series.

[2]*Ibid.,* p. 187.

was so settled was intended to be the form of all Christian societies for all time to come, different groups of Christians have at various times, separated themselves from the main body, and claimed, in some cases not without reason, to be recurring to a more primitive type.[3]

He adds, in summary, about the church:

. . . Its unaccomplished mission is to reconstruct society on the basis of brotherhood. What it has to do it does, and will do, in and through organization. At once profoundly individual and profoundly socialistic, its tendency to association is not so much an incident of its history as an essential element of its character. It spiritualizes that ineradicable instinct which draws man to man and makes society not a convention but a necessity. But the framing of its organization it left to human hands.[4]

(2)

The introductions provided by Bishop J. B. Lightfoot in his edition of the *Apostolic Fathers* (Macmillan, 1891) are brief. There is nowhere in them any mention of the idea of the restoration of an apostolically conceived church.

(3)

Gustav Kruger's exhaustive catalog of *Early Christian Literature* (Macmillan, 1897) gives room in its 400 pages for only brief comments on the contents and purposes of the writings of the Ante-Nicene church. In some instances, however, several pages of discussion are given to these themes in a single author. Out of this extensive study of the multiphased subjects of the writers in his field, Kruger makes no mention of the idea of restoring a normative, apostolic church.

(4)

The Christian Ecclesia, by F. J. A. Hort, has served since its publication in 1897 as a standard volume of reference in its field. It portrays the unfolding of the organization and authority of the primitive church and contains numerous insights that

---

[3] *Ibid.,* p. 216.
[4] *Ibid.,* p. 221.

are of value for our theme here. Departing in some measure from normative Protestant interpretation of the Good Confession, Professor Hort says:

In virtue of this personal faith vivifying their discipleship, the Apostles became themselves the first little Ecclesia, constituting a living rock upon which a far larger and ever enlarging Ecclesia should very shortly be built slowly up, living stone by living stone, as each new faithful convert was added to the society.

But the task thus assigned to St. Peter and the rest was not for that generation only. To all future generations and ages the Ecclesia would remain built upon them, upon St. Peter and his fellow disciples, partly as a society continuous with the Society which was built directly upon them in their lifetime, partly as deriving from their faith and experience, as embodied in the New Testament, its whole knowledge of the facts and primary teachings of the Gospel.[5]

However, the sharing of legislative authority with at least the elders, if not also of the whole church (Acts, chapter 15), the vacillation of Peter concerning the relations of Jews and Gentiles such that Paul accuses him of "acting a false part" (Galatians 2:13), the ambiguity of just who constituted the Twelve, the distinction between a Petrine gospel to the circumcision and a Pauline gospel to the uncircumcision, and the utter silence in Acts and the Pauline epistles about the four requirements of Christian neophytes proposed in Acts, chapter 15, are only a few of the problems that stand in the way of conceiving of an apostolic group building a once-for-all delivered church organization, as Hort's volume sees the matter. Indeed, as shown in the advice sent by the Jerusalem elders and apostles to Antioch, the author affirms "There is no trace in scripture of a formal commission of authority for government from Christ Himself. . . . The authority even of the Apostles . . . was moral rather than formal; a claim to deference rather than a right to be obeyed."[6]

[5]From *The Christian Ecclesia,* by F. J. A. Hort, pp. 17-18. Copyright 1897 by The Macmillan Co.
[6]*Ibid.,* pp. 84-85.

What we have seen in preceding sections dealing with the Fathers, wherein a distinctive way of life rather than distinctive organizational characteristics[7] were enjoined, is observed by Hort as being in the consciousness of Paul. He comments on Philippians 1:27 as an

exhortation to live a community life worthy of the Gospel of the Christ, one directed not by submission to statutes but by the inward powers of the spirit of fellowship; as St. Paul himself explains within the same sentence, "that ye stand fast in one spirit, with one soul wrestling together through the faith of the Gospel" (the faith which it teaches and inspires); and more fully still in the following section (2:1-11).[8]

Hort emphasizes and reiterates Paul's stress upon the unity of the universal ecclesia. The church was a very real entity to Paul and, despite his appreciation of the reality of divine grace and the unseen, "There is no indication that St. Paul regarded the conditions of membership in the universal Ecclesia as differing from the conditions of membership in the partial local Ecclesiae." As a conclusion of Hort's study of "gifts and grace," however, he says:

. . . At every turn we are constrained to feel that we can learn to good effect from the apostolic age only by studying its principles and ideals, not by copying its precedents.[9]

(5)

When we read the pluralized word in the title of George W. Richards' clear-sighted volume, *Christian Ways of Salvation*,

---

[7]A bit of caution in this generalization is submitted by a valued reader, Ralph G. Wilburn, of the College of the Bible, Lexington, Kentucky. He writes of "the resolute effort he made to align everything with apostolic institutions. His acceptance of the apostolic 'commands' of repentance and baptism, etc., was of course made very strong by a (contradictory) strain of irrational fideism in Tertullian's theology. See his tract on 'Repentance.' Tertullian's emphasis on apostolicity, of course, was at the center of his reply to the Gnostics, and the fact that he conceived of the apostolic episcopate as a greater authority than the apostolic canon or the apostolic creed is significant. . . . by Tertullian's day the transition in the conception of the church from personalism to institutionalism, was well under way. Indeed, Tertullian himself contributed greatly to the institutional development with his moralism, legalism, notion of penance, and his semistoic interpretation of the sacraments, especially the Eucharist."

[8]Hort, *op. cit.* p. 137.

[9]*Ibid.*, p. 169.

82

we are not surprised to find the same very significant (for our study) pluralized word in the heading of Chapter IV, "The Ways of the Apostles." Professor Richards has the historical insight to remember that when we speak of the primitive church we should mean its first few years. The organization of this truly primitive church was in a fluid, experimental state. The apostles and disciples "felt themselves in possession of the Spirit of Christ. This was the *new thing*—not a doctrine nor an organization, but a quality of life."[10] Such a life "would in due time create for itself an organization and an institution."[11]

Stephen's insistence that the new religion "will change the customs which Moses delivered to us" (Acts 6:14) was only one rock of conviction around which swirled the fluid forces seeking a form of words and of institutional organization for the new faith. Dr. Richards traces the "difference of views . . . among men who belonged to the same Christian fellowship."[12] "There was, at this stage, neither creed nor book as the object of faith. They trusted and hoped in the living Jesus, whom God raised from the dead and exalted into glory."[13] Much detail is given to show that in Paul's view "The church is primarily an organism, not an institution," and that as such its ordinances are "mystical and sacramental. . . . Baptism is clearly considered a miracle and a mystery. . . ."[14] In brief:

. . . Paul's interpretation of salvation as the transformation of man's sinful nature through the power of the divine Spirit proceeding from God in human form; his doctrine of the pre-existent Christ become man; the cosmological, historical and soteriological setting which he gave Jesus as the "man" from "heaven" and the "second Adam," the head of a new race; his conception of the Church and the sacraments as the bearers and channels of mysterious divine powers for man's redemption,—all these ideas were *original contributions of the Apostle to the Gentiles,* which super-

---

[10]George W. Richards, *Christian Ways of Salvation* (New York: The Macmillan Company, 1923), p. 85.
[11]*Ibid.*, p. 88.
[12]*Ibid.*, p. 92.
[13]*Ibid.*, p. 94.
[14]*Ibid.*, p. 110.

83

ceded the Jewish Christian messianism, made the gospel appeal to the imagination of Greek and Roman, and yet prepared the way for developments in Catholicism which were foreign to the spirit and purpose of Paul.[15]

This substantial volume finds no conception of a fixed ecclesiastical organization with unchanging rules of institutional life to have existed in the minds of the apostles, or the Ante-Nicene church. The author knows, of course, that "The different Christian churches have arisen because the founder of each was convinced that he had discovered a way of salvation truer to the way of Jesus and the apostles than the way of any of the existing churches."[16] What place, then, does organization and ecclesiastical machinery merit, in Christian life today? Dr. Richards answers:

. . . The church which, by virtue of its doctrine, organization, and life, most effectively sets forth Christ to men, and thus fills them with the Spirit; which expresses itself in works of faith, labors of love, and the patience of hope,—that church most adequately accomplishes the Christian task.[17]

(6)

The excellent book of Cyril C. Richardson, *The Church Through the Centuries,* makes no mention of the idea of an apostolic pattern of the church during the Ante-Nicene age (Chapter II)—nor is the idea noted elsewhere in the volume. An article by the same author in the *Journal of Religion* for October, 1937, entitled "The Church in Ignatius of Antioch" is a detailed study of its theme which brings forth no restoration concept. Indeed, Ignatius is rather an advocate of ecclesiastical evolution, not restoration, for it is in him that the rise of a three-order ministry takes place in Christian history.

---

[15]*Ibid.,* p. 111, italics added.
[16]*Ibid.,* p. viii.
[17]*Ibid.,* pp. 276, 277.

It is scarcely possible to exaggerate the importance for our study of the volume by Ernest F. Scott, *The Nature of the Early Church*. Its message can be epitomized in this paragraph:

In all times it has been recognized that the church must study the example of the early days, and seek, if possible to follow it. Too often, however, a false value has been placed on this example. It has been assumed that in all matters of government and institution the church must model itself on the primitive community. For that brief period at the beginning the church was uncorrupted. It guided itself in all respects by the instruction of Christ himself, and the one test of a true church is its similarity to that primitive one. On this point ecclesiastical controversy has always turned. Each denomination has sought to make out that it alone has remained faithful to the original model. The church of the Apostles was Episcopal or Presbyterian or Congregational, or was more akin to such irregular sects as the Plymouth Brethren or the Salvation Army. Every type of religious organization can be shown, without much difficulty, to have resemblances to the church of the New Testament. But we are now learning to see that all this discussion is beside the mark. The primitive model was one which never can be reproduced, for it answered to conditions which were altogether unique. The community had not yet called itself a church. It had no set order or government. It placed itself wholly under the control of the Spirit, which resided in the group as a whole and in each individual member. Such a community was possible only at the very beginning, when the church was small and was fired with a high enthusiasm. Even within the first year or two the primitive model had to be abandoned, and to return to it now would lead to no other result than sheer anarchy. We cannot revive the New Testament church, nor is this desirable. Jesus himself laid down no directions as to how his followers were to order their society. He only gave them a task to fulfill, and left them to discover for themselves how they might do so most effectually. Again and again the church must organize itself afresh, to meet the requirements of each new time, and according as it is best fitted to the time it gives meaning and reality to its message.[18]

Chapter V, "The Organizing of the Church," is especially instructive with regard to the theme of our study. The "good old days" of spontaneous service without organizational promotion and direction were obliged to give way to the methods of any growing society and to fix duties upon selected persons. "Competent officials had to be chosen, books had to be kept as in ordinary business. If these methods were neglected injustice was sure to happen, and the feeling of brotherhood, which it was the aim of the church to foster, could not be preserved."[19] New occasions taught new duties. Change of organization was as natural as life itself, answerable only to the claim of fulfilling the original purpose.

(8)

Currently, a book deserving and receiving a most careful attention is the Hoover Lectures for 1955, by John Knox, *The Early Church and the Coming Great Church*. Professor Knox observes, "However the goal of the ecumenical movement is to be reached, it will not be by the simple return to the primitive church."[20] This is his judgment upon the basis of his assessment of the historical sources which reveal the picture of the church in its early generation, meaning primarily the Ante-Nicene Fathers.

As we have seen in our firsthand examination of the Fathers, so does Knox find that "There was wide diversity in both cult and faith, and signs of tension and of actual division both within and among congregations are not lacking."[21] His important chapter on "The Growing Unity" sees the emergence of a new or Catholic church government which he terms "another type of church order,"[22] not as derived from the earliest

[18]From *The Nature of the Early Church*, by E. F. Scott, pp. 5, 6. Copyright 1941 by Charles Scribner's Sons. Used by permission.
[19]*Ibid.*, p. 105.
[20]From *The Early Church and the Coming Great Church*, by John Knox, p. 12. Copyright 1955 by Abingdon Press. Used by permission.
[21]*Ibid.*, p. 13.
[22]*Ibid.*, p. 121.

church of Jewish origin but from the later Gentile areas. The elder system, with congregationalism as its structure, he terms "too cumbersome" to be practical.

With regard to the specific theme of this section (Chapters II-IV) of our book, the use of the restoration idea by the Fathers, Knox sees them as the holders of an important authority of their own rather than the echoers of only an older authority. He illustrates it by the example of the normativeness of the New Testament. He says:

The only consistent position is that which recognizes that the New Testament is the creation, not of the first century only, but of the first several centuries of the experience of the church, and that the acceptance of it means the acknowledgment of a broader locus of the authority which ancient Christianity exercises in the church than the primitive community alone comprises.[23]

It is apparent, then, that the major scholars who know the Ante-Nicene Fathers see them not as advocates of a single or simple type of organizational restorationism, but rather as witnesses in behalf of a developing, ethical, spirit-led life. What we have observed in our examination of the Fathers is confirmed by these careful students—i.e., that the one thing the church forever was and must be restoring is the purpose and program of Jesus, a righteous way of life for men.

---

[23]*Ibid.*, p. 140.

CHAPTER V

Historic Applications of the Restoration Idea: Through the Middle Ages

I

Jesus was the first Christian advocate of the restoration principle. In Matthew 19:8 he appealed to a primitive, pre-Mosaic ethic or relationship to God as the basis of his new teaching about marriage. From that day to the present the Christian community has been periodically blessed—and occasionally plagued—by those who would call an erring people upward to the particular ideals promulgated in another day.

Our Lord further illustrated his restoration idealism when he insisted that he came "not to abolish but to fulfil" the Mosaic law. (Matthew 5:17.) There is an unmeasurable store of wisdom and instruction in what he meant in these well-known words. He was a restorationist, and the law of Moses with its detailed forms and observances was known intimately to every one of those who heard his words about fulfilling the ancient code; but there was not the slightest intention on the part of Jesus to retain the forms or even the institution, as such, into which he was born. As twentieth-century "Daughters of the American Revolution" would be horror-stricken to be caught in anything so revolutionary and custom-changing as the historic movement which gave them birth, so most modern advocates of Christian restoration would be aghast at a program similar in aim and spirit to that of the Nazarene, one that was concerned about life and motive and willing to let the forms and ceremonies survive or perish on the basis of their practical, teaching value. The universalism of Jesus and his thought of restoring religion in its essence to a non-Hebraic character were perceived by that brilliant intellectual meteor of World War I, T. E. Lawrence, author of *The Seven Pillars of Wisdom*. On pages 356-357 he says:

. . . Christianity was a hybrid, except in its first root not essentially Semitic. . . . Galilee was Syria's non-Semitic province, contact with which was almost uncleanness for the perfect Jew. Like Whitechapel to London, it lay alien to Jerusalem. Christ by choice passed his ministry in its intellectual freedom.[1]

The first serial correspondence in the New Testament, and probably the very first books in the Christian scriptures that were written, contain the inevitable theme of a restored faith. After Paul had made his personal sojourn with the church at Thessalonica, and had put his subsequent admonitions to its members in written form (1 Thessalonians), he was faced with the necessity of recalling to the minds of these early disciples the specific instructions that he had delivered in person. Their grand hope was in the expected return of Jesus, the imminence of which Paul emphasized at length in his first letter. When a few years passed and the second coming of the Lord was a theme for scoffers, the apostle endeavored to restore the faith of the Thessalonian Christians in this anticipated event, saying, "Now concerning the coming of our Lord Jesus Christ and our

---

[1]Used by permission of Doubleday & Co., Inc., publishers.

assembling to meet him, we beg you, brethren, . . . stand firm, and hold to the traditions which you were taught by us, either by word of mouth or by letter." Through the centuries there have been and in this present day there are those whose conception of the Christian faith almost wholly consists of the anticipation of the early coming of Jesus. This revival of a peculiar hope is one of the historic, continuing applications of the restoration principle, the vast and variegated panorama of which it is our purpose to view in part in these pages.

The renewal of an ethic, a special way of life, has been another recurring message of the preaching and teaching from the sourcebook of Christianity because such a program is in that book itself. Far-reaching movements within the church which have existed for centuries and absorbed the major interest of devoted men and women have been dedicated, at least in their beginning years, to the restoration of Christianity in terms of its ethical message and person-to-person relationships. The sermon of James, commonly called a "general epistle," is a scathing indictment of the misuse of wealth, of the ravages of lust, of vanity in possessions, and of conformity to the ways of the world. Pure religion, indeed, is specifically defined in this rule: "to visit orphans and widows in their affliction, and to keep oneself unstained from the world." This conception of Christianity as primarily an ethic ("What does it profit, my brethren, if a man says he has faith but has not works? Can his faith save him? . . . Faith by itself, if it has no works, is dead.") finds its primary support in the Sermon on the Blessed Life, from the lips of Jesus himself. Here are exalted the virtues of mercy, of peacemaking, of reconciliation, of personal righteousness which exceeds pharisaical formulae, of actions so honest that an oath is superfluous even unto sin, and of love even toward enemies who shall be opposed only by the power of prayer. With the backing of such authority as that of Jesus and his brother we are not surprised that again and again there arise movements in the world church calculated to give back to the Christian community some large measure of benevolent life-luster.

90

II

It is not our purpose in this chapter, however, to emphasize the restoration idealism of the New Testament period, but rather to observe how this basic philosophy of religion has worked through the succeeding centuries. How have men gone about the task of embodying the faith they gained from the Founder? When deviations from the true genius of Jesus' religion crept into the fellowship, how were the original conceptions recaptured? Elemental heroism and devotion like that of the Founder himself will come before us, and absurdity without limits will also appear. The historic applications of the basic urge to restore the original faith stand in rich variety.

Such an experience is not peculiar to Christianity. All religions have the same fundamental problems. For example, the volume by Dwight Goddard and others, *Laotzu's Tao and Wu-Wei*,[2] says:

. . . While Laotzu would find little in common with the busy, impertinent activities of so-called Christian statesmen building by statecraft and war, he would find much in common with Apostolic Christianity which held itself aloof from current politics and refused to enter the army, content to live simply, quietly, full of faith and humble benevolence.

As George Foot Moore further elaborates in his solid study of this theme, Laotzu was a true restorationist in that he would take man back to a presumed original state of nature.[3] Space here does not permit us to follow the intriguing path of this phase of our theme, known in literature as Romanticism, and having Rousseau as one of its most profound exponents.

The Shin sect of Japanese Buddhism also illustrates the regard for the original or primitive religious experience of the founder of the faith. The promised paradise of Jodo, which preceded Shin, was called the Pure Land. Shinran Shonin, originator of the new group, went on to promise reward in a True Pure Land,

---

[2]Copyright 1935. Used by permission of Coward-McCann, Inc., publishers.
[3]See *History of Religions* (New York: Scribners, 1914), Vol. I, Ch. II, especially pp. 50f.

not by works of merit but by faith alone. However, not to be outdone in the matter of restoring the true faith, Shin was followed very shortly by Nichiren, whose sect proposed to reinstate Gautama Buddha in his rightful position.[4] Numberless individuals have devised their own restoration movements.

The place of the restoration hope in the Old Testament is integral to its structure. There is no opportunity to expound this theme here, but every student of the ancient scriptures is obliged to treat it. Of course, since the Old Testament period precedes the Christian era, any use of the idea of reconstituting the organization of a former religious life would have no bearing on our study problem. In passing, however, it is interesting from the standpoint of the universality of the restoration hope to see how constantly it was present in the religious life of the old Hebrews. We may demonstrate this simply by noting the strong ecclesiastical primitivism in Ezekiel. His cultic system was designed to purify the society and thus ensure the return of Yahweh to Jerusalem. Julius Bewer says the prophet worked out the basic principles of his system so thoroughly that it stood objectively before him in a vision.[5]

III

In Chapters II-IV we traced the ever-present restoration passion through the period of the Ante-Nicene church, to A.D. 325. This constant desire to recapture the faith and experience of the Founder and his disciple band did not flame briefly for three centuries only to die suddenly. It remained—and yet persists—throughout the succeeding centuries.

Indeed, there are many other instances of the appeal to a primitive religious way of life in the same peroid as that of the Ante-Nicene Fathers apart from the Fathers themselves. Gnosticism, which in time was adjudged untrue and injurious to Christianity, had as its purpose the restoration of *some* men to the

---

[4]See *The Religions of Mankind,* by Edmund D. Soper (New York: The Abingdon Press, 1940), pp. 255-259.

[5]In *The Literature of the Old Testament* (New York: Columbia University Press, 1940), p. 179. J. M. Powis Smith and William A. Irwin, however, say chapters 40-48 look back rather than forward. See *The Prophets and Their Times* (Chicago: University of Chicago Press, 2nd edition, 1941), Chapter X.

higher world—the noumenal world, Kant would have said—to which they belonged by virture of the divine spark given to them in creation. For many years Gnosticism maintained itself within the church as a claimant to orthodoxy. A. C. McGiffert says of Marcion, brilliant leader of the Roman Christian Gnostics, "It was his desire to restore the original gospel in its purity and with this in view he devoted himself earnestly to the study of the epistles of Paul and other primitive Christian writings."[6] Irenaeus' writings against the movement, about the year 180, did not prevent the gentle and learned Clement of Alexandria from calling himself a Christian Gnostic as late as the third century.

When Victor was bishop of Rome (190-198), he was confronted with the problem of a school of thought, denominated as the Alogi, headed by the Theodoti and including a certain Artemon. Before the latter was excommunicated, he put up as his defense the claim that in his doctrine (styled dynamic monarchianism) he "held the primitive faith of the Roman church."[7]

Much more successful in obtaining a following for the recapture of primitive Christian faith and living were the Montanists. Their founder was Montanus of Phrygia, A.D. 130, and others in the movement were Tertullian of Africa[8] and perhaps the famous martyrs Perpetua, Felicitas, and their companions (202). If ever there was a determined effort to enjoy once more the old-time religion, this was it. The slogan of Montanism might well have been: "The restoration of primitive Christianity, its doctrines, its ordinances, and its fruits." In brief, the primary concern of this group, entirely orthodox in theology, was to revive belief in the imminence of the second coming of Jesus, chaste and simple living, and the primacy of the prophet in the public work of the church. (See Ephesians 4:11.) Only with great effort did ecclesiasticism, or the dominance of the bishop, overthrow these zealous early puritans.[9] The essence

[6]From *A History of Christian Thought*, I, 59. Copyright 1932 by Charles Scribner's Sons. Used by permission.

[7]F. J. Foakes-Jackson, *The History of the Christian Church*, to A.D. 461 (8th edition, Chicago: W. P. Blessing Company, 1927), p. 169.

[8]For some detail on Tertullian and his teaching, see Sec. I in Chapter II.

[9]See A. C. McGiffert, *op. cit.*, I, Ch. IX; F. J. Foakes-Jackson, *op. cit.*, pp. 224-226.

of their claim was that they were reviving New Testament Christianity in its uncorrupted form.

Toward the close of the third century Paul of Samosata, eminent in political office and in theology, fathered a movement in the thought of the church for the recapture of primitive Christianity's faith in a personal God which he felt had been destroyed by the abstruse speculations of the school of Alexandria. The fact that Paul was condemned by the Synod of Antioch in 268 does not detract from his lofty conception of Christ but only exhibits the numerical dominance of the Logos advocates who outvoted him. Right or wrong, Paul believed that he was restoring the true conception of Jesus prevailing in the primitive Christian community.[10]

Not to be confused with the followers of Paul of Samosata were a numerous people called Paulicians, from their cleaving to Paul the Apostle, whose later military prowess gave them a substantial history of Armenia and the Balkans. Arising in the seventh century, they called themselves Christians simply and adhered to the New Testament with the exception of those letters ascribed to Peter. Opposing the externality of current Catholic life they rejected images, relics, and monasticism. However, they became dualists with Gnostic elements and probably contributed much to the origin of the Bogomiles and subsequently to the Cathari of Southern France.

IV

For want of space here, and because illustrations from later times are more available in extant literature, we shall move from the Nicene and post-Nicene era to the medieval period.

E. H. Broadbent, of England, in his book on *The Pilgrim Church,* calls attention to the great significance of a work written by an unknown figure of the eighth or ninth century and entitled *The Key of Truth.* Much of its content could have been used unchanged by any advocate of restoration movements of a thousand years later. Central to the purpose of this in-

---

[10]See McGiffert, *op. cit.,* I, 242.

fluential publication was not only its repudiation of the apostasy of the state church, but also a delineation of the simplicities of faith, order, worship, and life of a true church, patterned on apostolic principles. "Conversion and church membership were for those who had believed, repented, and been immersed. . . . A room devoid of furniture, other than a plain table with a white cloth on which were laid the emblems of the Lord's Supper and a copy of the Gospels provided adequate paraphernalia for the congregational expression of the faith."[11] So successful, for a time, was this restoration program that the hatred of it by the established Christian institution was said to be "more bitter than that of pagan Rome in the apostolic age."

It is difficult for modern men to reconstruct in their minds the condition of the Roman Catholic church in the eleventh and twelfth centuries, especially with regard to its unity and disunity, its authority and lack of authority in divers places. The consolidation of its adherents into the fairly unified body which they represent today and the wielding of its united power through the use of modern communication give an exhibition of strength, authority, and unity which was scarcely dreamed of in the minds of Middle Age popes. Arnold of Brescia could escape any inconvenience arising from his condemnation by the Council of Sens in 1141 by carrying on his reform in France. Here, as Ellen Scott Davison indicates, "The sentence of Sens was not approved . . . and no bishop was found to execute the harsh judgment of the Council against Arnold. . . . Hyacinthus, later a cardinal, evidently an influential man, espoused Arnold's cause. . . . Moreover, conditions in France were unfavorable to united clerical action. A heated controversy centered around a bitter struggle for the see of Bourges and diverted attention from all minor issues. King and pope, noble and monk, stood arrayed against each other."[12]

After this Arnold spent seven years in Rome, associating with a civil revolutionary party, preaching against the luxuries and vices of the bishops, and charging: "The Pope was no Pope

---

[11]C. H. Phillips, in the *Christian Standard*, July 7, 1951, p. 10.
[12]*Some Forerunners of St. Francis of Assisi*, by Ellen Scott Davison, p. 36. Privately printed, 1907.

because he was not an apostolic man and a shepherd of souls but a man of blood, who maintained his authority by killing and burning; a tormentor of the churches; and oppressor of the innocent, who did nothing in the world but feed on flesh and fill his coffers and empty those of others."[13] Popular sentiment in the papal city was strong enough to support the reformer in these charges and to keep him safe over a period of years.

Unorthodox movements were to be found in many other places, challenging the power of the Roman church. In 1030 the nobles of Milan offered conversion to Catholicism or death by fire to a number of sectarians of Monteforte near Turin. Many, including the countess of the place, sprang into the flames.[14] In 1052 Henry III felt obliged to hang certain New Manicheans in Goslar; but new advocates of the same ideas appeared about 1090 at Agen, and again in 1115. In the Netherlands from 1115 to 1124 the enthusiast Tanchelm, "ecstatically venerated by the multitude, moved about with a bodyguard of armed men, with a banner carried before him, and bearing a naked sword ready to cut down all unbelievers."[15] Moeller adds, "The spreading contempt for the church even after Tanchelm's death compelled Norbert to appeal for help against the disburbances excited by him." Lack of space forbids to tell of the monk Henry who, about 1101, succeeded in arousing some of the lower clergy, as well as Bishop Hildebert, against the luxurious higher clergy; of Peter of Bruys, whom Peter of Clugny and Abelard designated as "the most dangerous of all the heretics who threatened the ecclesiastical cultus"[16]; and of Endo de Stella, condemned to imprisonment by the Council of Rheims in 1148. What is important is that new movements for reform were frequently arising, often to flourish for many years without hindrance from the weak central hierarchy, and sometimes under the protection of local kings or princes despite the specific disapproval and even long-standing excommunication on the part of the Roman church.

[13]*Ibid.*, p. 41.
[14]See *History of the Christian Church, Middle Ages,* by Wilhelm Moeller, Copyright 1898-1900 by The Macmillan Company. Vol. II, p. 383.
[15]*Ibid.*
[16]*Ibid.*, p. 385.

V

In the face of such conditions it is not surprising that there were those whose reading of the scriptures of the church discovered a profound disparity between the primitive apostolic life and that which then obtained, especially in ecclesiastical high places. When we consider that the times were soon to give birth to the prolific movements of the friars and remember with how much ardor these men sought ideals which changed the very temper of the church, we might expect to find restoration concepts in the new monasticism. Cardinal Newman, however, observed that "The monk proposed to himself no great or systematic work beyond that of saving his soul."[17] With the possible exception of Hildebrand and the Cluniac movement, monasticism had little interest in reforming the church or the state. It is true that there was a species of restorationism integral to the Franciscan ideal, limited to the desire to restore apostolic poverty, simplicity, and personal virtue.[18]

An excellent instance of a restoration movement within a restoration movement is to be seen in the origin of the Capuchins. They arose from the persistence of a Matteo di Bassi, "a man of no intellectual powers, but endowed with more than the usual obstinacy of the Italian peasant." From the same province as Saint Francis, he proposed that all the brethren of the Order should obey the rules "to the letter, to the letter, to the letter." He restored the use of a pointed hood, instead of the then fashionable rounded one, and demanded the revival of the saint's custom of getting sermons from conversation with the people instead of from books. Says Lindsay, "This old Franciscan preaching was restored by the Capuchins, and they did more than any others to bring the people of Italy back to the discredited Church."[19]

---

[17]See *Evolution of the Monastic Ideal*, by H. B. Workman, p. 12. Copyright 1913 by C. H. Kelly.

[18]In 1953 there was dedicated in Chicago's Loop a Franciscan church described as "the most impressive ecclesiastical edifice in the city." One wonders what must be thought of it by Saint Francis, who wrote in *The Mirror of Perfection* that his followers should "build small churches, for they ought not to make great churches, neither to preach to the people, nor for any other reason, since their humility is greater...."

[19]From *A History of the Reformation*, by T. M. Lindsay, II, p. 509. Copyright 1906 by Charles Scribner's Sons. Used by permission.

Amid the welter of a richly variegated adaptation and modification of Roman church ideals, as well as distinct heresies (opposing, perhaps, only a few of the practices of the church), there were to be found certain Apostolics,[20] whose appeal for church authority was to the scriptures rather than to an official succession or tradition belonging to the Roman hierarchy. Davison says:

Efforts to restore primitive Christianity, to follow literally the commands of Christ and the teaching of the Apostles in daily life and in religious observance were very numerous in the eleventh and twelfth centuries. The conceptions men formed of the essence of Apostolic Christianity varied widely. The fundamental motive of all was the same: they would live as Christ taught men to live; they would conform their worship to that of the little group of believers who first followed Him in far away Palestine. Arialdus and Waldo, Arnold and Francis, agreed in basing the apostolic life on evangelical poverty. But Waldo wished to sweep away all doctrines, all religious observances, which were not found in the Church of the apostolic age; Arnold believed that the vicar of Christ should not be a secular prince, and assailed the whole vast fabric of the temporal power of the Church; Arialdus tried to purge the Church of simony, to teach the priests to lead pure lives; Francis saw clearly his own duty—to be poor, as Christ had commanded, to help suffering humanity, while he upheld the Church as an institution.[21]

VI

Material on the attitude toward the scriptures on the part of the Albigenses and Cathari is not readily obtainable. The customs and cult practices of these "New Manicheans," as they are commonly classified,[22] have captured the interests of most commentators upon them. This is not surprising, for these Western sects (excepting the Waldenses) were true cult kin of the Eastern Euchites and Bogomiles, who may be traced back to the earlier Paulicians of Armenia, Mesopotamia, northern Syria,

---

[20]For a brief summary of the general subject, see article "Apostolics," in *Encyclopaedia Britannica*, 11th edition, Volume I, pp. 204, 205.

[21]Davison, *op. cit.*, p. 14.

[22]See article, "New Manicheans," in *The New Schaff-Herzog Encyclopedia of Religious Knowledge*, Volume VIII, pp. 143f.

Thrace, and later Bulgaria. The dualistic tradition of Persia imparted certain ascetic and orgiastic elements into Albigensian and Cathari practice. These features have seized the imagination of historians with regard to the Western apostolics who existed in northern Italy and southern France during the eleventh and twelfth and even into the thirteenth centuries, with the result that their devotion to the restoration principle has been lost to our sight.

The great movement of Cathari at Albi consisted of New Testament Christians of an unusual species, for they carried their Manichee dualism, which saw material creation as evil, to the point of identifying the Old Testament Jehovah with the evil one, Satan. Therefore they discarded the Old Testament and stood on the New Testament alone. By emphasizing certain aspects of early Christian life many peculiarities were authorized by these purists, including the prohibition of marriage, the inculcation of other ascetic practices, as well as an involved metaphysical teaching. This latter item would "hardly have won converts in numbers sufficient to enable Catharism to supplant the Church in southern France and to weaken it seriously elsewhere."[23] It was popular condemnation of the luxurious living of the clergy in contrast with the New Testament teaching and practice of simplicity, which won the great Catharian following.

Various examples of the preaching of these eleventh- and twelfth-century Apostolics remain. The principal tenets of Peter of Bruys and Henry of Lausanne were, that

they denied the efficacy of infant baptism because Christ said "Believe and be baptized," and a child cannot believe; Christ's body and blood are not offered in the Sacrament, nor did God command that the Sacrament be celebrated; all sacrifices and prayers for the dead avail nothing; churches and altars are unnecessary, for prayer before a stable is as efficacious as that before an altar.[24]

Certain heretics of Cologne were discovered by Everwin, Provost of Steinfeld, claiming that the Roman establishment had

---

[23]Davison, *op. cit.*, p. 19.
[24]*Ibid.*, p. 20.

lost its primitive character and thus ceased to be a Church of Christ. "All the observances of the Church which were not founded by Christ and the Apostles in direct succession from Him they called superstitious."[25] Unlike the stricter Cathari, these Apostolics of Cologne did not prohibit marriage nor deny the validity of the Old Testament. Davison estimated that it was "through their attempt to restore the apostolic Church that they gained their hold on the popular imagination."[26]

Everwin reports that there was a second group of self-designated "Apostolics" at Cologne—presaging, perhaps, the modern divisions among Bible Christians, by "their mutual disagreement and contention,"[27] as he says of them. "They said in their own defense," he adds, "that this heresy had existed secretly from the time of the martyrs to our own day. . . ."[28] Their positive message was an appeal for apostolic poverty and simplicity in life and worship. They repudiated the Roman church, and originated one of their own (with a hierarchy, bishops, and a pope!) in which they founded their customs on a literal interpretation of the teaching and practice of Christ and the apostles.

VII

Usually, though not correctly,[29] associated in historical treatises with the Albigenses are the Waldensians, who are much more truly to be known as Bible Christians than is the case with the Albi purists whose origin and cult practices show such an

[25]*Ibid.*, p. 22.

[26]*Ibid.*, p. 23.

[27]Saint Bernard de Clairvoux, *Cantica Canticorum,* translation of Samuel J. Eales (London: E. Stock, 1895), pp. 389, 391.

[28]Davison, *op. cit.*, pp. 23, 24.

[29]One of the few near-source books in this field in English is Jean Paul Perrin's volume, *Luther's Forerunners* (title page reading "The Bloody Rage of that Great Antechrist [*sic*] of Rome and his superstitious adherents, against the true Church of Christ, and the faithful professors of his Gospel"), printed at London in 1624. The second half of his work is a history of the Albigenses, and begins as follows: "The Albigenses, which we are to speake of in this history, differ nothing at all from the Waldenses, in their beleefe: but they are onely so called of the Countrey of Albi, where they dwelt, and had their first beginning. The Popes have condemned them as Waldenses; the Legates have made warre against them, as professing the beleefe of the Waldenses; the Monkes Inquisitors, have formed their Proces and Indictments as against Waldenses: The people have persecuted them as being such, and themselves have thought themselves honored by that title, upon the assured knowledge that they had of the puritie of their doctrine, being the selfsame with the Waldenses: In respect whereof, many Historiographers call them Waldenses." (pp. 1, 2, *The First Booke of the History of the Albigenses.*)

affinity with Eastern Manichaean precedents. The Waldenses had a commonplace and uninvolved origin in the experience of one man. Says Jean Paul Perrin in his volume of 1624:

> This was about the yeare of our Lord a thousand one hundred and threescore, at what time . . . Peter Waldo a citizen of Lions shewed himselfe most couragious. . . . He was in high esteeme for his learning and pietie, as also for his great bountie toward the poore. . . . Many Historiographers do write, that he had a resolution to leade an unblameable life, approaching as neare as he could to that of the Apostles. . . .[30]

As with most apostolics, the point of departure from the Roman church life announced by the Waldenses arose in a practical rather than a doctrinal consideration—the matter of primitive Christian economics.[31] "From the very first they adhered with the extremest rigidity to the minutest and most literal precepts of the Bible."[32] The monk Rainerius charged:

> that the first lesson that the Waldenses give to those whom they winne to their Sect, is this, that they teach them what the Disciples of Christ ought to be, and that by the words of the Gospell and the Apostles, affirming, that they only are the Successors of the Apostles, that imitate their life.[33]

The passage goes on to charge that "the Pope, the Bishoppes and Clergy, that possesse and injoy the riches of this world, and seek after them, follow not the examples of the Apostles," but the important point is Rainerius' complaint about, and seeming disparagement of, the simply scriptural basis of action. It was well known by those who opposed the Waldenses that "the said Pastors were thoroughly exercised in the Scriptures."[34]

---

[30]Jean Paul Perrin, *Luther's Forerunners* (London: 1624), "The First Booke," pp. 2, 3.

[31]It was so in other instances of revolt against the established church. Shortly after this, in England, Robert Grosseteste (b. 1175), forerunner of Wiclif, opposed the hierarchical absolutism imposed with such severity by Innocent III. "It was the corruption, rather than the theory, of the church which first aroused his antagonism. The mainspring of all his activity was always his devout and untiring solicitude for the salvation of men's souls." W. E. Garrison, "The Preparation for the Reformation in England Before Wiclif," B.D. dissertation, University of Chicago, 1897, p. 20.

[32]Article, "Waldenses," *The New Schaff-Herzog Encyclopedia of Religious Knowledge*, Vol. XII, p. 243.

[33]Perrin, *op. cit.*, "The Second Booke of the History of the Waldenses," p. 2.

[34]*Ibid.*, p. 36.

Waldo did what the critical and persuasive Arnold of Brescia never accomplished—he founded and perpetuated a separate church based on apostolic ideals.[35] The ex-heretic Sacconi testified that the Waldensians claimed that their own was the true Church, and "the Roman Church is no Church of Christ, but a Church of Malignants."[36] This church, the Waldensian, exists today, "the oldest extant Protestant group in the world."[37] As with reformers in other churches and centuries, "they had no thought of leaving the church and did not anticipate its opposition, but Peter Waldo was refused papal approval. In 1183 they were excommunicated. In 1207 the Waldenses found a refuge in the Cottian Alps in northwest Italy, and the valleys of that region are still the principal center of their life and work."[38]

Waldo performed one unique service for the development of heresy, or Bible Christianity, as one may choose to call it: he provided the Bible in the vernacular of his people. Before his full break with the Roman church he employed two priests to render the scriptures into French, one translating while the other wrote. "By the hit-or-miss translation made by the priests for him," says McNeill, "Waldo provided for medieval religion a new dynamic. Soon he attracted followers who multiplied the written vernacular scriptures and preached them widely."[39] Persecution scattered the Waldenses to far places, and with them went the scriptures. "It was their arsenal and the basis of their influence. They brought a biblical influence into numerous earlier and later sects with which they mingled—Cathari, Humiliati, Arnoldists, Spiritual Franciscans. . . . Through his popularization of the Bible his influence is vastly wider than his sect. Luther's Bible met a demand which had been aroused by the Waldensian propaganda. Calvin's first religious publication was an introduction to the new French translation for the

[35]For a careful discussion of the claim that Arnold founded a distinct sect, see Davison, *op. cit.*, pp. 45-54.

[36]From *Inquisition and Liberty*, by G. C. Coulton, p. 189. Copyright 1938 by W. Heinemann.

[37]Pamphlet, *A Miracle of Protestant Survival*, p. 2.

[38]*Ibid.*

[39]From *Makers of Christianity*, by John T. McNeill. Copyright, 1935, by Henry Holt and Company, Inc. By permission of the publishers.

Waldenses by his cousin, Olivétan, in 1535. Waldo thus appears to have held a good deal of the future in his hand."[40]

IX

Spiritually akin to, and later identified with, the undertaking of Waldo, was the movement of the Humiliati. "Between 1179 and 1201," says Davison, "apostolic Christianity had become a recognized force. Innocent III realized that the Church, beset by enemies who fought for conscience' sake, needed to organize all the enthusiasm and religious zeal she could command within her own ranks."[41] Arising from an ancestry reputedly going back to the time of the Emperor Henry II (who was in Italy in 1004 and 1014), and growing into a third, or nonclerical, order within the church, they seem to have received holy orders and claim to have been granted a rule by Saint Bernard in 1134. "The earliest known facts are that in 1176 a grant of land was made to the Humiliati near Milan, and that their right to hold land was assured in 1186 by Pope Urban III."[42] Upon petitioning the pope, three orders of Humiliati were given Rules in 1201.

There were certain "false Humiliati," however, who did not abide within the limits of ecclesiastical orthodoxy and remained apart from those who were content with Roman church rule. "The Humiliati, whose reconciliation with the church was assured by Innocent's careful policy, departed from the spirit of the movement, which was essentially an apostolic one."[43] The order fell into disrepute and was abolished in 1560. "The other Humiliati, false according to Innocent III, true to their convictions at great cost, were lost to sight among the Apostolic heretics who abounded in Lombardy. They had much in common with Arnold of Brescia, and may easily have coalesced with his disciples." Too, "They were naturally swept along with the Waldensian portion of the apostolic movement."[44]

---

[40]*Ibid.*, pp. 149-150.
[41]Davison, *op. cit.*, p. 56.
[42]*Ibid.*, p. 58.
[43]*Ibid.*, p. 68.
[44]*Ibid.*, p. 69.

From an entirely different sector we may note another instance of the claim of possessing primitive purity in church life and organization. A Chinese Nestorian in 1287 arrived in Rome on an embassy from the Mongol Kahn and the patriarch of Seleucia-Ctesiphon. He said: "As for us Orientals, the holy apostles taught us, and up to the present we hold fast to what they have committed to us."[45]

X

One of the substantial historical works on the period preceding the Protestant Reformation is C. Ullmann's *Reformers Before the Reformation,* in two volumes.[46] A careful reading of this record turns up scores of citations of individuals and whole movements dedicated to the restoration of primitive Christianity. Of the period we have just noted, embracing Arnold of Brescia and others, Ullmann says, "An attempt was accordingly made to bring back Christian life, in all its branches, to its primitive purity, and to the simplicity and dignity of the Apostolic times. Apostolicity in fact became the watchword of the parties dissatisfied with the Church."[47]

First in point of time among the distinctly theological reformers may be listed John of Goch, born about the beginning of the 15th century in the Duchy of Cleves. His education may have been gained at one of the institutions of the Brethren of the Common Life. Reacting against the scholastic theology of his day, Goch emphasized the importance of a biblical base in Christian doctrine, and heralded a new age in his effort "to seek in the simple and really quickening truths of primitive Christianity that refreshment, purity, and vigour which were necessary for new productions."[48] Setting him in his historical era, Ullmann makes this comparison:

. . . Wickliffe had assailed the mendicant monks, the usurpations of the Hierarchy, and the perversion of the doctrine of the sacra-

---

[45]From *The History of Yaballaha III,* translated by James A. Montgomery. Copyright 1927 by Columbia University Press.

[46]Translated by R. Menzies (Edinburgh: T. & T. Clark, 1855.)

[47]*Ibid.,* I, 8.

[48]*Ibid.,* I, 36.

ments. Huss had sketched the beau-ideal of the Church, of the Episcopacy, and of the Priesthood, and had held it up before a corrupt Hierarchy and clergy, that they might behold it and blush. It was chiefly against the corruptions of the clerical body, and the abuses of indulgence, that John of Wesel took the field. With the fiery eloquence of a prophet Savonarola attacked the moral degeneration of all ranks, of the people and the nobility, both in the state and the Church; while Erasmus poured his pungent wit upon the stupidity and folly, the superstitions and abuses of his age. None of them all, however, penetrated so deeply into the general spirit of the Church, which was the basis of all the mischief, the root from which the unchristian or antichristian tendencies grew, or depicted these tendencies with such precision as the silent, calm and thoughtful John of Goch.[49]

Goch's *Treatise on the Four Errors Touching the Gospel Law* employs, as its concluding criticism of the prevailing Christianity of inventions and forms, an appeal to the "primitive and inward spirit of freedom."

Goch was a brave radical for his day in demanding an essential equality between the episcopal and presbyterial offices, but he did not advance to the recognition of the universal priesthood of all believers, which was the contribution of the Protestant reformation. He defended the sacerdotal nature of the priestly order, arguing "there is the return it involved to what is primitive and apostolical." He opposed the rule of bishops, however, insisting that their reputed succession was on "the custom and enactment of the Church, but not in respect of the primitive institution of the Sacraments, and the Divine appointment."[50]

There was born in 1482 at Alost (Aelst) in Flanders one who carried the theological findings of Goch into the arena of activity, with ensuing personal discomfort. Cornelius Graphaeus was eminent in most of the arts and sciences of his day, and an intimate of Erasmus. He was the center of a circle in Antwerp which sought a purer embodiment of the Gospel. He published Goch's book, *On the Liberty of the Christian Religion,*

[49]*Ibid.*, I, 83.
[50]*Ibid.*, I, 128.

about 1521, with a Preface of his own, fiery in spirit, and thereby gained imprisonment at the hands of the Inquisitors. As an older man he recanted, but in the period of his bravery and enthusiasm he was a power for reformation. As solvent for the ills of Christianity he prescribed "a return to Apostolic simplicity and eternal truth." In the Preface to a smaller work of Goch, *Epistola Apologetica,* Graphaeus insists Christians must "with honest minds embrace the pure doctrine of Christ, drawn from the wells of Holy Scripture, and not from the marshy puddles of Thomas or Aristotle. That is what we honor and will endeavor to restore."[51]

Gregory of Heimburg was a man of broad interests, noble family, and much learning, having attained the doctorate in laws about 1430. He entered the service of Aeneas Sylvius when the latter was a leader of the opposition party in the church. The German Gregory retained his convictions and came to poverty and exile. Personally heading an embassy of protest at Rome in 1446, Heimburg boldly challenged the claims of his former patron, and wrote a treatise entitled *An Admonition Touching the Unjust Usurpations of the Popes of Rome, addressed to the Emperor of all Christian Kings and Princes.* The second part of the treatise contrasts the then current modes with primitive Christianity. Seduced by opportunity Aeneas Sylvius abandoned his early idealism and in 1458 became Pope Pius II. When the pope demanded that the city of Nuremberg deliver up Heimburg as an excommunicate, the latter expanded his reforming views in public addresses and written works, some of which are extant and testify to his restoration idealism and zeal.

Much could be included here about Jacob of Juterbock, active in the middle 15th century against indulgences, in opposition to which he held up the practice of the primitive church.[52]

The same observation would be valid concerning John of Wesel, who was incensed by the commercialization of Roman years of jubilee, which caused the popes to repeat them at the profitably diminishing periods of 100, 50, 33, and 25 years.

[51]*Ibid.,* I, 137-142.
[52]*Ibid.,* I, 254.

"We read," says Wesel, "the discourses of Jesus Christ the Son of God recorded in the four Gospels," but in them "not a word is said of Indulgence." As to the reputed Treasury of Merit from which such grants were claimed to be made, says John, "that any such agreement has ever been made by Jesus with the ministers of the Church is not stated in the Gospel."

The ethical note in Wesel's restoration philosophy was strong. He argued that in the pastor's relations with the people "helpful sympathy ought to be directed no less to their spiritual than their temporal good, and more especially, according to the pattern of Jesus and the Apostles, to the care and succor of the poor. . . . The Redeemer promises the glory of the apostolic name to those who shall abide in his word." Indicting the avaricious hierarchy of his day Wesel was fearless in condemnation. He proclaimed, "The man from whom I hear nothing of Christ's righteousness, and in whom I perceive no insight and knowledge, I refuse to confess as a master, I own not in him the authority of a bishop, nor reverence him as a pastor." Concerning the conduct of worship, he charged, "Behold, Christian brother, how the whole face of the primitive Church of Christ has been changed!"[53]

Wesel was careful to distinguish his conception of the Church of Christ and his acceptance of the visible Catholic Church, the former divine and the latter a work of man with relative authority. His view was that the true church was not an institutional affair, so that even the apostles were quite limited in power and importance. John was Christocentric, insisting that "just as at the first Christ alone gave the new law, and the Apostles had no sort of authority to enact new statutes for the Church, so does Christ still act and do all that is necessary for salvation, and needs no substitute to do for him things which he cannot himself accomplish."[54] This removes John of Wesel from the ranks of those who founded their faith upon apostolic rules and precedents.

[53]*Ibid.*, I, 258, 261, 290, 319, 322.
[54]*Ibid.*, I, 358.

This is not the place for an extended exposition of the nature of what may be termed pantheistic mysticism, but at least a brief notice of the theme and a representative advocate of the position must be given. We saw in Section II of this chapter that Laotzu proposed a return to a presumed original and pure state of man. This ideal found expression in Christianity at various times, including the period we are now examining.

The industrious communal religious societies—the Béguines and the Béghards—suffered a change of interests and a loss of their good name for productive contribution to society and morals during the fourteenth century. Felix Hammerlein's treatises chronicle the decline, telling of their growing absorption in speculations about the second coming of Christ, and their consorting with the Brethren and Sisters of the Free Spirit. They were numerous enough in some sections of Europe to be termed a common plague, as they went about in distinctive garb, holding secret meetings, and charging the corrupt church with its sins. "Their own professed object was to restore the pure primeval state, the divine life of freedom, innocence, and nature." Man, they said, was naturally good prior to the fall, and could return to that perfect condition. They were charged with arranging Paradises where sexual promiscuity was encouraged. Undergirding their program was a philosophy of pantheistic mysticism, which had supported protest movements in various periods of history. Their restorationism was of a very thorough-going species, and should not be overlooked in any survey of this idea through the ages.

Different in kind was the mysticism of John Ruysbroek, born about 1293, but it too led him to a program of restoration of what he understood by primitive Christianity. He was another of the forerunners of the great and constructive movement of the Brethren of the Common Life, themselves precursors of the Protestant Reformation, and notable restoration advocates.

Ruysbroek's theistic mysticism sought after apostolicity "not so much in external forms as rather in the spirit, and in the whole tenor of the life." He insisted that no priesthood nor office can save, but only a "life corresponding to the Spirit and pattern of Jesus Christ."[55] The "mysticism" of Ruysbroek derived from his understanding that Christ had bequeathed counsels to all Christendom concerning a higher state of perfection, but relating to the practical matters of poverty, and chastity of soul and body. He praised early monasticism for embodying these virtues, and did not fail to show the decline ensuing. Ruysbroek's greater work, however, consisted in his personal influence upon others who were to excel him in restoration philosophy and practice, John Tauler, and Gerhard Groot.

Gerhard Groot (Geert Groete, or de Groot, Gerhardus Magnus) was a practically minded as well as devout Dutchman born in 1340, famed as the founder of the Brethren of the Common Lot, an organization "conformed as far as the circumstances of the times would permit to the apostolical pattern . . . imitating the Church at Jerusalem" in the sharing of earnings and property. His was the kind of loyalty to an institution which loved it so much that while he was accredited with supporting its every part and function, and was long adjudged thoroughly orthodox, his very devotion became a fire which would burn away untrue elements in the structure. "The primitive apostolical Church shone in his eyes as the model of perfection. In it he found a piety and fervor of zeal which, in his own days, he no longer beheld. Hence he desired to see, if not all, yet at least the more important, rites remodeled after its pattern." A more spiritual priesthood was one of his aims, and he specifically charged that "consistently with the pattern of the primitive church, you cannot hold a plurality of benefices."[56]

Florentius Radewyns, born about 1350, carried forward the societies and gathered about him young men of good training who devoted themselves to "a pious, simple, and apostolical life," charging each to "comply with the same habits of the Lord."[57]

The very title of the principal work of Thomas Hamerken, better known as Thomas á Kempis (born 1380), *The Imitation*

[55]*Ibid.*, II, 31, 51.
[56]*Ibid.*, II, 70, 71, 75, 76.
[57]*Ibid.*, II, 82, 85.

of Christ, is an index of his ethical or mystical restorationism. Ullmann notes that Thomas "uses the life of Christ, even to the minutest point, as a pattern for himself and others"—with the usual personal interpretation. For example, Thomas argued that we are justified in writing Christian books only because Jesus "stooped down and with his finger wrote on the ground," from which, says the Middle Age author, "it is pleasing to hear that Jesus could read and write, to the end that the art of writing and zeal in reading pious books may delight us the more."[58]

It may be admitted, as Ullmann observes, that "Thomas is not intentionally a Reformer," and we find in him no positive scheme for institutional reconstruction. However, he was a part of that growing body of able men of pre-Reformation years who saw the incongruity of the church as they knew it in comparison with what the church was designed to be, according to the Scriptures.

When the Brethren of the Common Life gained solid appreciation from the multitudes they served, certain monks filed formal charges of heresy against them on the simple grounds that they were religious but didn't belong to an established order. In other words, they lived like the New Testament Christians (as they specifically claimed) but didn't observe some of the accumulated forms of historic Christianity. John Gerson defended the Brethren and gained an acquittal for them in 1418 on the grounds that Jesus himself would be excluded from a "religious" life by such a measurement.

The period we have been examining in this section has been rich in advocates of the mystical type of restorationism. This is frequently allied with the ethical emphasis, but neither of these has carried a lasting concern for institutional or formal primitivism. Our account would be bulky if it gave notice to the host of genuine mystics, true restorationists all of them, who crowd the Middle Age period. They were not primarily proponents of a message for the church as an institution, however.

---

[58]*Ibid.,* II, 148.

Ullmann chronicles the lives of many pre-Reformation mystics, characterizing their individual-centered programs as follows:

... Man, as a creature originating directly from God, who is one, longs to return, according to his capacity, back to the undivided unity. The afflux strives again to become a reflux: and only when all things in him have become wholly one in and with God, does he find entire peace and perfect rest. .... What belongs to God by nature, man must acquire by grace. To this end the pattern of Christ has been given to him.[59]

Concluding our survey of pre-Reformation advocates of species of restorationism, we may cite John Wessel (not to be confused with John Wesel, born perhaps in the same decade but who died in 1481, eight years before John Wessel). It was as a theologian that he participated in the disintegration of the foundation assumptions of the Roman church institution. Its assertion of the Gospel's dependence upon the church he denies, saying "It is for God's sake that we believe the Gospel, and for the Gospel's sake that we believe the Church and the Pope." This was a repudiation of Augustine's orthodox affirmation: "I would not believe in the Gospel unless the authority of the Catholic Church induced me to do so." *(Contra Epistolam Manichaei.)*

John Wessel nowhere lays down a precisely defined notion of the church, unfortunately for our purposes. He affirmed its unity, defined in terms of a communion of saints. He was not an iconoclastic reformer, but said he believed *with* the Church, not *in* it. Thus its living tradition had a value for him, and he could accept the papacy as a practical but dispensable agency. Wessel's impingement upon our subject is obvious in his pre-Lutheran suggestion of the primitive Christian practice of the priesthood of all believers, with clergy created by a free compact, having authority only for edification.[60]

---

[59]*Ibid.,* II, 208.
[60]*Ibid.,* II, 482-495.

CHAPTER VI

Historic Applications of the Restoration Idea: The Modern Period

I

The Protestant Reformation under Luther was not a democratic movement based on trust in the common people. It was certainly far removed from any flavor or contamination of communism, Christian or otherwise. Luther was afraid of the common man. "He opposed the Anabaptists on principle and not from motives of policy. While he came from the ranks of the working classes, he never really had any sympathy with them. He was a bourgeois, and, as was also true of Calvin and Zwingli, the Reformation in his hands represented a revolt of the lower aristocracy against the higher."[1]

[1] From *Pioneers of Christian Thought*, by F. D. Kershner. Copyright © 1930, used by special permission of the publishers, The Bobbs-Merrill Company, Inc.

The restoration of New Testament practices for all important phases of religion did not appeal to Luther. As Lindsay says, he wanted a "conservative reformation."[2] When Andrew Bodenstein of Carlstadt took the side of the Swickau Prophets and urged upon the town of Wittenberg in 1522 an ordinance embracing such primitive Christian practices as a common treasury, simple or lay dress for the ministry, and changes in the worship forms, Luther returned to the city to preach for eight successive days, and "the plague was stayed." As one scholar puts it, ". . . the reformers aimed to reform the old Church by the Bible; the radicals attempted to build a new Church from the Bible."[3] The "radicals" would have preferred to say that they were not building a "new" church, but restoring the original one.

However, the basic proposition of the Protestant Reformation was the authority of the Bible, so one would expect and does find appearing the idea of the revival of the idealism and practice of New Testament religion. It came to public advocacy on the part of no less a personage than Philip, landgrave of Hesse, leading layman of the Reformation.

Philip was not afraid of democracy, and his treatment of the common people was so sympathetic that it spared his lands from the ravages of the Peasants' War. Unlike Luther, he did not denounce the Anabaptists. In 1526 he summoned a Synod at Homberg, including representatives of the towns, and presented a scheme for ecclesiastical government eliminating canon law and advocating officebearers "who ought to conform as nearly as possible to those mentioned in the New Testament Scriptures." They ought, he said, "to be chosen by the congregation, and set apart by the laying on of hands, according to apostolic practice." Luther remonstrated strongly, however, and the plan was abandoned. As Lindsay says, "There is no place for the democratic or representative element in the organisation of the Lutheran churches."[4] With such a denial of

[2]From *A History of the Reformation*, I, 318.

[3]From *The Anabaptists, Their Contribution to Our Protestant Heritage*, by R. J. Smithson, pp. 14-15. Copyright 1935 by James Clarke & Co., Ltd. Used by permission.

[4]From *A History of the Reformation*, by T. M. Lindsay, I, 415-16. Copyright 1906 by Charles Scribner's Sons. Used by permission.

democracy and fraternity, we are not surprised at the title of a modern Lutheran work, *Why a Lutheran Should Not Attend Any Other Church,* nor that its reason for this attitude is "because the Lutheran church is the old original church."

II

The Reformation led by Calvin was more akin to the restoration idealism that we have seen running like a continuous, colored thread through the woven strands of Christian history. Rejecting Luther's consistorial form of church government, and the Roman medieval ideas of ecclesiastical rule, Calvin and the Reformed advocates would "return to the principles which they believed to be laid down for them in the New Testament."[5] The great Genevan wanted, for example, to revive the observance of the Lord's Supper every week.

Calvin's immense learning embraced an intimate knowledge of the voluminous writings of the Ante-Nicene Fathers, and this fact may have had some bearing on his desire to restore not just New Testament practices but also the distinctive features of the church of the first three centuries—to him the "golden period" of Christian history. Zwingli differed from Calvin on this point, contending that the pattern of the church when it lacked sympathetic emperors for civil rulers should not be compared with the more Christian era under friendly state auspices. This was particularly true with regard to excommunication, in which "the German Swiss Reformers took the one side, and the French Swiss Reformers took the other; and the latter were all men who had learned to reverence the usages of the Church of the first three centuries, and desired to see its methods of ecclesiastical discipline restored."[6] The town council of Lausanne resented the effort to remove its medieval church practices in favor of *"any new-fangled fashion borrowed from the primitive Church."*[7]

The story of the Reformation in Switzerland is replete with appeals to the authority of New Testament church practices.

---

[5]*Ibid.,* II, 7.
[6]*Ibid.,* II, 111.
[7]*Ibid.,* II, 113. Italics added.

It was so at the Synod of Zurich, 1538, when more frequent celebration of the Lord's Supper was requested, "according to the practice of the primitive Church."[8]

In France the famous conference at Poissy, 1561, heard the gospel of apostolic Christianity. Protestantism was being advocated by men of noble birth, and an impressive company witnessed the proceedings, presided over by the king with his mother, Catherine de Médicis, his brothers, and princes of the blood present. The Chancellor's speech before the Roman Catholic theologians argued that the main difference between them and the Protestants was that the latter "wished the Church to be reformed according to the primitive pattern."[9]

Professor Lindsay insists that the reason why the Netherlands chose presbyterianism, or the Reformed organization, as its preferred type of church government—a choice decided upon while Alva was pressing in full persecuting fury against the Lowlands Protestants—was because presbyterianism was "the revival of the government of the Church of the early centuries while still under the ban of the Roman Empire."[10] Thomas Cartwright was a representative spokesman for the Reformed faith when he insisted that the presbyterian polity was the one divinely authorized system. Thus one is not surprised that some years ago the Presbyterian Board of Publication in America issues a volume entitled *Which Is the Apostolic Church?* that affirmed: "We regard it therefore as put beyond all reasonable doubt that, of all the churches now existing in the world, the Presbyterian church comes nearest to the apostolic model."

The Reformation in Scotland soon felt the need of a confessional standard, and the resulting document of 1560 was entitled the *First Book of Discipline,* or the *Policie and Discipline of the Church.* Professing to go "directly to Scripture for the outlines of the system of Church government,"[11] the authors produced a program employing ministers, teachers, elders, dea-

---

[8]*Ibid.,* II, 123.

[9]*Ibid.,* II, 186.

[10]*Ibid.,* II, 271. See also T. M. Lindsay, *The Church and the Ministry in the Early Centuries,* 2nd ed. (London: 1903), pp. 198, 204f, 259, 330, 339.

[11]Lindsay, *op. cit.,* II, 305.

cons, superintendents, and readers, working in kirk-sessions, synods, and general assemblies.

In England the Protestant Elizabeth succeeded to the crown late in 1558, and one problem of the ecclesiastics was how to get Mary's Roman Catholic laws off the books in time for a Protestant observance of Easter in 1559. The enabling proclamation said, among other things, that the holy Sacrament should be received "under both kinds, according to the first institution, and to the common use both of the Apostles and of the Primitive Church."[12]

This action was only a logical outcome of the direction of religious thought established by Henry VIII. He abolished the conferring of the papal pall, arguing that it was not given in the England of pre-Norman days, and had no precedent in the early church. As Wakeman says, "The appeal was no longer to be solely to the historical precedents of the English Church but to primitive antiquity itself."[13] In 1534 Parliament passed a resolution denying the primacy of the pope, and asserting that Scripture contains no evidence of such a prerogative. "In this it is not difficult to discern the hand of Cranmer, whose mind tended in the direction of basing the justification of the Reformation theologically upon Scripture and antiquity."[14] John Macleod says of the Puritans of England, "The goal for which they were making was a return of the church to the apostolic pattern. This they sought to reach all along the line not only in Faith but in Order and Discipline and Worship."[15]

At the close of the sixteenth century Thomas Hooker composed the classic defense of the Anglican system against the Puritans, whom he felt were going too far in restoration zeal. Said he of them: "They hold that one only law, the Scripture, must be the rule to direct in all things, even so far as to the taking up of a rush of straw." The seventh book of his famous *Ecclesiastical Polity* defends episcopacy on the basis of

[12]*Ibid.*, II, 399.
[13]From *The History of the Church of England,* by H. O. Wakeman, 10th ed., p. 217. Copyright 1923 by Rivingstons.
[14]*Ibid.*
[15]From *Scottish Theology*, pp. 6, 7, 1943, Publishing Committee of the Free Church of Scotland.

the Bible and tradition. Citing that the church for 1500 years had been under "the sacred regiment of bishops," he employs this testimony of time in observing: "If therefore we did seek to maintain that which most advantageth our own cause, the very best way for us and the strongest against them were to hold even as they do that in Scripture there must needs be found some particular form of Church polity which God hath instituted, and which for that very cause belongeth to all churches, to all times."[16] The materialistic fetish of an unbroken succession in church office, while overshadowing other consideration in his view, needed the bolstering of an original, scriptural example in the primitive church.

During the early sessions of the Westminster Assembly the Dissenting Brethren had objected to the establishment of a national church on a Presbyterian model. Charged with being obstructionists, they sought to justify their position by issuing *An Apologetical Narration*. There were two major principles, they asserted, upon which they had proceeded in their thinking concerning the outward arrangements of the church.

"The supreme rule," which they had followed, ". . . was the primitive pattern and example of the churches created by the Apostles."[17] They are willing to concede, as Henry Burton was later to acknowledge, that "no such model is left in the New Testament as was given to Moses in the Old"[18]; yet they could not "but imagine that Christ hath ever been as exact in setting forth the true bounds and limits of whatever portion of power he hath imparted unto any (if we of this age could attain rightly to discern it) as he hath been in ordering what kind of censures and for what sins, . . . which we find he hath been punctual in."[19]

When the historic contest for control in the Church of England was nearing the climax which issued in the Toleration Act of 1689, Edward Stillingfleet was Dean of St. Paul's, in

---

[16]Chapter X.

[17]*An Apologetical Narration*, London, 1643, p. 9.

[18]*Conformity's Deformity*, London, 1646, p. 9.

[19]Thomas Goodwin and Philip Nye in Preface to John Cotton, *The Keys of the Kingdom of Heaven*, London, 1644. This episode in Dissenting Brethren history was presented by Winthrop S. Hudson, in "Denominationalism as a Basis for Ecumenicity: a Seventeenth Century Conception," *Church History*, March, 1955.

London. In 1,662 he published his *Eirenicon,* saying:

It would be strange indeed the Church should require more than Christ himself did, or make other conditions of her communion than our Savior did of Discipleship. . . . Without all controversie, the main in-let of all the distraction, confusions and divisions of the Christian world hath been the adding of other conditions of church-communion than Christ hath done.

The English philosopher, John Locke, wrote in 1680 a "Defense of non-conformity" which he did not then publish. Locke was a member of the established church, but in the "Defense" he argued that the primitive church and its practices should be the criterion for a reconsideration of the establishment. In 1689 his famous (first) *Letter Concerning Toleration* clearly affirmed his position:

But since men are so solicitous about the true church, I would only ask them here by the way, if it be not more agreeable to the Church of Christ to make the conditions of her communion consist in such things, and such things only, as the Holy Spirit has in the Holy Scriptures declared, in express words, to be necessary to salvation?[20]

Hugo Grotius (the Latin and popular form for his Dutch name Huig de Groot), 1583-1645, was an Arminian of Holland who achieved such fame as a jurist that he is still called "the father of international law." High among his concerns, however, was the problem of church union—the sad side of which he knew intimately through his grievous sufferings during intolerant Calvinist rule. Grotius wrote two books on ecclesiastical peace, and in the introduction to one of them said:

I understand that Christ had willed that all named after him and trusting in his salvation should be one with the Father, and the beauty of the primitive church did greatly please me, at that time when she was without doubt catholic, since all Christians . . . remained in one communion.

---

[20]The Works of John Locke (London, 9th ed., 1794), Vol. V, p. 15.

Before turning to some of the lesser-known advocates of primitive Christianity in the era inaugurating the modern church, it is pertinent to recall that Roman Catholicism also felt obliged to defend itself on the basis of the then newly popularized scriptures. Frederick C. Grant says:

. . . there were two Reformations, the Protestant and the Catholic. The latter has been called the "Counter-Reformation," but the name is unfair; its mainspring was not mere opposition to Protestantism, but was an effort to restore and reaffirm the position of the church in the Middle Ages (which was, perhaps naturally enough, thought to be identical with the form it possessed at the beginning).[21]

In order to remove from Protestantism any claim to being a restoration movement, and to obtain this virtue for the Roman church, Pope Pius X in his encyclical *Editae saepe Dei* (May 26, 1910) said of the reformers, ". . . they dared to call this violent rebellion and this onslaught of faith and morals a restoration; and to call themselves restorers of the ancient discipline. In fact they were corruptors. . . ."

III

Outside of the main stream of the Protestant Reformation were many smaller rivulets of Christian life flowing in the same general direction. Summarizing this period, Atkins and Braden say: "The common folk of North Europe developed a simple piety, largely independent of sacraments and the church technique, and fashioned on the way of Jesus. It began to recapture the primitive spirit of the Gospels which had been long overlain, and to manifest itself in charities and the humane concern for poverty and suffering."[22] In church government and practice, however, "while some sat very loose to the letter of Scripture, others insisted on the most literal reading and application of Biblical phraseology."[23] Of the anti-Trinitarian

---

[21]Copyright 1936 Christian Century Foundation. Reprinted by permission from *Christendom*.

[22]*Op. cit.*, p. 476.

[23]Lindsay, *op*. cit., II, 424.

119

party, perhaps the most distinguished leader was the Spaniard, Miguel Servede (Servetus), whose volume published in 1553 was entitled *Christianismi Restitutio*. Thoroughly sympathetic with the Anabaptists, Servetus would restore believer's baptism. As his peculiar restorationism, however, he would defer baptism, after the example of Christ until the thirtieth year.[24]

An emphatic ethical restorationism was evident in the program of the "Melchiorites," followers of Melchior Hoffmann, whose understanding of the New Testament involved communistic sharing. Of the Anabaptists as a whole Lindsay says, "their main thought was to reproduce in their own lives what seemed to be the beliefs, usages, and social practices of the primitive Christians."[25] After reviewing again the variety of individualism of the Anabaptists, the author repeats once more: "The one idea common to all was, that the Christians of the sixteenth century were called to reproduce in thought and life the intellectual beliefs and usages of the primitive Christians."[26] The account of these times is sprinkled with tales like that of Hans Hut, who would appear at a peasant home, spend the night converting the family to New Testament Christianity as he understood it, baptize the folk, and go on never to return. Of course, among such wandering preachers and prophets there was the most extreme individualism, leading to many varieties of "New Testament" religious practice and emphasis.

The tragic fate of the city of Münster had its origin in the work of Bernhard Rothmann, a reformed Humanist and Lutheran. As his thought about religion developed he rejected infant baptism, which resulted in a public disputation sponsored by the town magistrates and participated in by Roman Catholics, Lutherans, and reformers. Going on from his success in the debate, Rothmann advocated New Testament forms of charity. "His sermons and his life had an extraordinary effect on the rich as well as on the poor. Creditors forgave debtors, men placed sums of money in the hands of Rothmann for distribution. There was no enforced communism, but the example of

[24]*Ibid.*, II, 439.
[25]*Ibid.*, II, 439.
[26]*Ibid.*, II, 441.

the primitive Church in Jerusalem was followed as far as possible."[27]

English Congregationalism produced thinkers and martyrs for the restoration cause. Robert Browne, says the historian Bates, "was the first Englishman who dared openly to support the Anabaptist position that the church should return to the pattern of Primitive Christianity with autonomous congregations organized by voluntary agreement or covenant." Modern democracy, both in religion and politics, was struggling to be born here. The persecution and forced removal of the Brownists "was the first example of what was to become one of the most astonishing phenomena of the period—the emigration of whole parishes led by their pastors in search of religious freedom denied them in England but possible in Holland, and later in parts of America."[28]

One almost forgotten advocate of the restoration of primitive Christianity was Daniel Defoe, the novelist, an earnest non-conformist layman, whose book, *Robinson Crusoe,* of world-wide popularity, was published in 1719. It may surprise the reader to discover how pointedly Defoe used this vehicle to convey his religious faith. Briefly told, the point is that the savage Friday, saved from cannibals, was instructed in Christianity by the hero of the book, and was enabled to become a full Christian without benefit of clergy, state church, or other aid beyond what was learned from the Bible that Robinson Crusoe had salvaged from the wrecked ship. Thus did Defoe give a rejoinder in part for his having been pilloried for three days and imprisoned nearly two years because he published a satirical pamphlet about the harsh treatment of Dissenters.

IV

Early in the course of American colonization the freedom of thought and life exercised by Separatist minds came to voice in a Mr. Ambros Martin who was tried in Massachusetts "for calling the church covenant a stinking carryon & a humane

---

[27]*Ibid.,* II, 457, 458.
[28]From *American Faith,* by E. S. Bates, p. 76. Copyright 1940 by W. W. Norton & Company, Inc.

[sic] invention & saying he wondered at God's patience" because "the ministers did dethrone Christ & set up themselves; he was fined £10 & counselled to go to Mr. Mather to bee instructed by him."[29] Somewhat later but in quite an identical spirit the eminent John Adams of American revolutionary days was numbered among the religious reformers because he revolted against the machinery and high society control of the church and asked, "Where do we find in the Scriptures . . ." the nonessentials of Christian life to which he objected.[30]

One of the most original thinkers of North America was Roger Williams, founder of Providence Plantation in Rhode Island. He was the author of a novel turn in religious speculation, especially as it relates to the theme of this volume. Organizer and minister of the first Baptist church in America, he soon became disturbed about his right to administer church ordinances, "conceiving that a true ministry must derive its authority from apostolic succession and, therefore, he could not assume the office of pastor." In time he concluded that the church was so corrupt that there could "be no recovery out of that apostacy till Christ shall send forth new apostles to plant churches anew."[31] This idea of restoration by divine initiative of a new apostolate has gained few followers in history.

In 1696 William Penn published a little book, *Primitive Christianity Revived,* the purpose of which was to show that the program of the Quakers was the plain gospel message of the primitive church. Another book in 1711 bore exactly the same title, but was the work of a William Whiston and caused him to be banished from the University of Cambridge.

The restoration interests of Solomon Paine are evident in the title of his book, published in 1752, *A Short View of the Difference between the Churches of Christ and the Established Churches.* Paine, a Separatist of Canterbury, Connecticut, was opposing the then growing movement to establish an Anglican episcopate in America—or any other established church.

---

[29]D. W. Howe, *The Puritan Republic* (Indianapolis: Bowen-Merrill Co., 1899), p. 40.

[30]Preserved Smith, *The History of Modern Culture* (New York: H. Holt & Co., 1930), II, 451.

[31]From *The Story of Religion in America,* Revised, by W. W. Sweet, p. 70. Copyright 1950 by Harper & Brothers. Used by permission.

Among the estimated two hundred "Edens" or Utopian societies that established colonies in North America there were many that justified their programs wholly or in part on principles of the New Testament. Numerous books have been written about these communities, one of the more recent works being that of the late V. F. Calverton, *Where Angels Dared to Tread*.[32] It would double the bulk of this volume—and add no little to its roster of freakish movements—if we should describe in detail the specific claims of these societies to the effect that they were reproducing the manner of living enjoined in the New Testament. To select from Calverton's array of ideal societies only one example of New Testament Restorationism, the Labadists may be cited. They established the pioneer communistic society on this continent, Bohemia Manor, which perished before 1727. To their search after a "pure and primitive Bible Christianity" they added practices derived from their belief in and following of the "inner light." Dr. Carl R. Fish, in his history of *The Rise of the Common Man*, records a later revival of the communistic communities. "Between 1840 and 1850 more than forty communistic projects were attempted . . . based on the desire to return to the simplicities of early Christianity, and on philosophic concepts. . . ."[33]

We observed in the previous chapter that the ancient Laotzu desired to direct men to a life in accordance with a presumed original state of nature. In 1731 Tindal brought out his book, *Christianity as Old as the Creation*, contending that genuine Christianity is identical with the religion of nature. He says: "The business of the Christian dispensation was . . . to restore, free from all Idolatry, the true primitive, and natural Religion, implanted in Mankind from the Creation."[34]

An unusual functioning of the restoration principle was exhibited by the Skoptzi sect of Russia, cited in Karl A. Menninger's book on suicide, *Man Against Himself*. The purpose of the Skoptzi sect was to take literally the injunction of Matthew

---

[32]Indianapolis: Bobbs Merrill Co., c. 1941. Other good works include Gilbert Seldes, *The Stammering Century*, and C. W. Ferguson, *The Confusion of Tongues*.

[33]P. 189, Copyright 1944, by the Macmillan Company.

[34]M. Tindal (London: MDCCXXXI), pp. 347, 348.

5:29-30—"If thy right eye offend thee, pluck it out, and cast it from thee: for it is profitable for thee that one of thy members should perish, and not that thy whole body should be cast into hell. And if thy right hand offend thee, cut it off, and cast it from thee: for it is profitable for thee that one of thy members should perish, and not that thy whole body should be cast into hell." (KJV.) Selivanov, the founder of the sect, taught that man's offending member was the organ of procreation.

Not only self-castration but also baptism by fire was practiced by the Skoptzi sect. Selivanov "baptized himself by fire" by mutilating himself with a blazing iron, and likewise baptized others. All members were urged to gain new converts toward the goal of the 144,000 which would usher in the blessed day. Anyone who brought in twelve mutilations was given the distinction of apostleship. Whole communities were sometimes secured to the faith, one consisting of 1,700 souls. The important volume by B. Z. Goldberg entitled *The Sacred Fire,* tells the story of this sect. It is related how many converts performed the necessary operation on themselves, but halted in the process because of pain or fear. To take care of this situation, the sect established different degrees of mutilation and designated those of one as being of the "Greater Seal" and those of another as being of the "Lesser Seal."[35]

The Skoptzis were not the only Russians to lay claim to a restoration of true religion. The dominant Orthodox Church, long the national religious institution, through Nicholas N. Glubokovsky, in modern times, has said:

Orthodoxy is the authentic and primitive Christianity of our Lord Savior and of his apostles. Orthodoxy successively preserves and holds it, adapting it and developing it amid various historical conditions. It results therefrom, that in its inward thrust, Orthodoxy thinks itself as Christianity in its primordial completeness and uncorrupted entirety.[36]

---

[35]The antiquity of this religious idea is well known, having appeared in Phrygia and Syria long ago, and being present in modified form in the Flagellantes or Penitentes of New Mexico. J. J. M. DeGroot, the eminent scholar in the field of Chinese studies, cites related practices in that land.

[36]From "Orthodoxy in Its Essence," in *The Constructive Quarterly,* a Journal of the Faith, Work and Thought of Christendom, ed. by Silos McBee. Vol. 1, No. 2. June, 1913. Dr. Glubokovsky was a professor at the Imperial Orthodox Ecclesiastical Academy, St. Petersburg, Russia.

Although Mr. Wakeman, author of a previously cited volume, wrote from a distinctly Anglican point of view, there is an eloquent passage in which he praised the nonconforming John Wesley as an eighteenth-century Saint Francis. In part, he wrote, "To live the life of Jesus Christ in the world was the common object of both—of the one through imitation of His poverty, of the other of His sinless perfection." After many sentences of praise and others of censure, he summarizes the purpose of the Methodist founder as "the desire to revive the usages of the primitive Church."[37] It is interesting to note that Wakeman challenges Methodism not on the basis of scripture but by the standards of "Catholic theology" and claims about church organizational rights from "the earliest centuries"—which were scarcely primitive. In this connection, the common Methodist belief in the New Testament character of its life and organization is to be seen in a book by Nathan Bangs, *An Original Church of Christ; or, A Scriptural Vindication of the Orders and Powers of the Ministry of the Methodist Episcopal Church.*[38] This is a logical outgrowth of the faith of Wesley expressed in his letter of September 10, 1784, to Coke and Asbury in North America: "As our American brethren are now totally disentangled both from the state and from the English hierarchy, we dare not entangle them again either with the one or the other. They are now at full liberty simply to follow the Scriptures and the primitive church."

Methodist advocates were prompt to exploit this claim to primitive Christianity. Benjamin Lakin, a Maryland-born preacher who labored many years in Kentucky and Ohio, wrote in his diary, December 3, 1795, that he believed the Methodist-Episcopal system of overhead control "agrees with the government of the Apostles."[39] In the *Great Carrollton Debate* (Ditzler vs. Graves), published in 1876 by the Southern Baptist Publication Society, Proposition Four reads: "The Methodist Episcopal Church at Carrollton, Missouri, possesses the

[37]Wakeman, *op. cit.*, p. 440.
[38]New York: T. Mason & G. Lane, 1837.
[39]From *Religion on the American Frontier*, Vol. IV, *The Methodists, A Collection of Source Material*, by W. W. Sweet, p. 212.

scriptural characteristics of a church of Christ. . . ." On page 922 Dr. Ditzler affirmed, "God raised up and thrust out the Wesleys and their coadjutors to save Protestantism, to save society, and restore Christianity."

Yet Methodism itself later had to be restored—if we may believe the historian of a body that split off from it, the Nazarenes. Of the latter group he says, "Both in head and in body the church is solid for the historic faith of Christianity as it has come down to us from Jesus and the Apostles."[40]

The intellectual or theological distance between much Lutheran thought about the church and salvation, which is medieval to the core, and that of Anabaptist and post-Enlightenment religious conceptions, may be seen by examining the clear expressions of N. F. S. Grundtvig, nineteenth-century exemplar of Danish Lutheranism. Commenting on a sermon by Grundtvig preached July 24, 1825, Begtrup says:

In this sermon Grundtvig for the first time makes known his conception of the *Apostolic Confession of Faith* as the unalterable, completely authoritarian testimony concerning the true Christianity, given by the living Church and independent of statements of Scripture.[41]

Here is a species of restorationism entirely different from anything previously presented in this survey. What the great Dane wanted was akin to the desire of the ancient Papias (Chapter II, Section III), for he would build upon a living voice or tradition, and restore nothing of a written code earlier than the Apostles creed. In another work Grundtvig says:

. . . The characteristic content upon which the early Christian Church built, by which it was distinguishable not only to its enemies but especially to its friends, and which undeniably must

[40]From *A History of the . . . Church of the Nazarene,* by J. B. Chapman, p. 35. Copyright 1926 by Nazarene Publishing House.

[41]It was July 31 before Grundtvig put forth this view polemically (the July 24 sermon was the older view of Grundtvig, which he revised July 31), in a "preaching" on "The Response of the Church." Dr. J. Knudsen, of Grandview Seminary, Des Moines, Iowa, a Danish Lutheran institution, has checked these references and ideas. See *N. F. S. Grundtvigs Udvalgte Skrifter* ved Holger Begtrup (Kobenhavn: Gyldendalske Boghandel, Nordisk Forlag, 1906), IV, 386f. See also Dr. Knudsen's article, "Beyond the Sacred Page," Journal of Theology of the American Lutheran Conference, September, 1940.

be found in every church which justly is called Christian, this, I claim, is found . . . wherever the apostolic confession of faith is made the exclusive condition for admission into the Church and where a saving power corresponding to the creed is attributed to the means of grace, Baptism and Communion.[42]

Or, to be quite specific, Grundtvig adds, "We have a Christian Confession of Faith which is so far from being exclusively founded on the Bible that, on the contrary, it is not at all founded on the Bible."[43]

Professor Klemmer of Allegheny College has pursued studies in the rise of American academic church history and has noted that the earliest American publications in the field were almost entirely devoted to the first three centuries, especially the first. He indicates that they were mostly efforts to prove by the norm of the Apostolic Church the validity of universalism, unitarianism, infant or adult baptism, presbyterian, congregational, episcopal or papal church polity. One suggestive title, for our study, cited by Professor Klemmer, was Coleman's *Apostolical-Primitive Church, Popular in its Government and Simple in its Worship* (1844).

The most recent history of the Mormons, written by a sociologist, says that they "offered claims to combine a restoration of primitive Christianity . . . with modern revelation from on high."[44] Parley P. Pratt, early Mormon leader, designated its founder, Joseph Smith, as "Elias, the Restorer."

We should not make the mistake of assuming that the restoration principle is solely Protestant in character and interest. We have seen that it appears in all religions and ages. It should be noted that this basic idea of religious refreshment and cleansing of the institution has its advocates in Roman Catholicism. The so-called Roman Catholic modernism movement was an appeal to the primitive faith of the church. Fathers

[42]Nik. Fred. Sev. Grundtvig, *Kirkens Gienmaele* (Kjobenhavn: Wahlste, 1825), p. 24, translated for this work by Dr. Kundsen.

[43]*Ibid.*, IV, 528.

[44]From *The Mormons*, by Thomas F. O'Dea, p. 2. Copyright 1957 by University of Chicago Press and used by permission. See also pp. 5, 20, 133f, 137, 142 and 225 for other references to Mormonism as a restoration movement.

Loisy and Tyrrell may seem to have made submission to Rome, but they did so only in company with an affirmation of faith in essential Christianity. The latter wrote:

. . . Any interpretation of papal infallibility which finds the organ of Catholic truth in the miraculously guided brain of one man; which renders futile the collective experience and reflection of the whole Church, destroys the very essence of Catholicism. . . . To interpret the Church's collective mind is the office of bishops, councils, and popes; as it is the office of a judge, not to make, but to interpret, the law. He is below it, not above it. . . . They speak *ex cathedra* so far as they say what she says.[45]

This is restorationism of a most thoroughgoing kind, but finds its meaning, of course, in the conception of a living, growing, or biological nature of the church, as compared to the normal Protestant use of the standard or norm theory of the institution and its characteristics.

While this book is, as far as the writer has learned, the most extensive investigation of its theme, it is not the first to recognize the universal sway of the restoration principle in religious life and organization. Early in the eighteenth century in Scotland the operation of the restoration idea was proclaimed by John Glas, Robert Sandeman, Robert and James Alexander Haldane, and Greville Ewing. In their congregations "the order of the primitive churches came to be progressively established in proportion as the understandings of this people in the Scriptures were enlarged." In 1805 J. A. Haldane published a volume with this long title: *A View of the Social Worship and Ordinances Observed by the First Christians, Drawn from the Scriptures Alone; Being an Attempt to Enforce Their Divine Obligation; and to Represent the Guilty and Evil Consequences of Neglecting Them.* Among the chapter titles we note:

Chapter I—There is reason to presume that the New Testament contains instructions concerning every part of the worship and conduct of Christian societies, as well as concerning the faith and practice of individuals.

[45]From *Through Scylla and Charybdis,* by George Tyrrell. Published 1907 by **Longmans** Green & Co. and used by permission.

128

Chapter II—All Christians are bound to observe the universal and approved practices of the first churches recorded in Scripture.

When the Haldanes brought out the volume they believed sincerely that infant baptism was the approved New Testament practice. Later they swung with equal sincerity to the belief that believer's baptism by immersion alone had apostolic authority.

The first of many founders of cults in Southern California was William Money, popularly known by such titles as "Bishop," "Doctor," and "Professor." He, too, made his primary religious appeal through the idea of restoring primitive Christianity, and published, some time after his arrival in Los Angeles in 1841, a book entitled *The Reform of the New Testament Church.* A Scotsman, he married a Mexican woman, and organized a cult composed largely of "native Californians," which he termed "The Reformed New Testament Church of the Faith of Jesus Christ." He built his home at San Gabriel in the form of a wierd oval structure, the approaches to which were guarded by two octagonal edifices made of wood and adobe. Born, as he contended without proof, with "the likeness of a rainbow in the eye," he died with a well-authenticated "image of the Holy Virgin above his head, an articulated skeleton at his feet, and a well-worn copy of some Greek classic within reach of his hand." The present writer, a former resident of Los Angeles, would not overlook the fact that Mr. Money once prepared a map of the world entitled "William Money's Discovery of the Ocean" on which San Francisco, a community he detested, was shown poised on a portion of the earth that he predicted would soon collapse, precipitating the city into the fiery regions. His death in 1880 robbed him of the satisfaction of seeing his word of doom partially fulfilled in the great earthquake of 1906.

V

Considering our theme in a chronological order, Christian Science may next be seen as an instance of grasping after some phases of a restored New Testament Christianity. One of its authorized manuals says this religious regimen is "designed to commemorate the word and works of our Master, which would reinstate primitive Christianity and its lost element of healing."[46] An official publication of the society affirms "the essential unity between the polity or government of the Church of Christ, Scientist, and the early Church."[47]

In the matter of terminology, the prize for restoration zeal should be given to the present-day denomination in England which takes as its name the Bible Pattern Church. It is listed in the current magazine, *Pentecost,* as a constituent member of the World Fellowship of Pentecostal Churches. In the United States, some related award could go to the denomination which carries the name "the Church of the Bible."

Next, consider the Dukhobors!

Not interested in the Dukhobors? Perhaps never heard of them, or only as a sect of Russian fanatics in Canada who fight off the census-takers, burn schoolhouses and occasionally go in for nudism in (of all places!) Saskatchewan? But wait. There is more to it than that. The record of this strange group includes such material as this: a seventeenth century defection from the Russian Orthodox Church in search of pure, simple, non-institutional "primitive Christianity"; a community that carried the principle of non-violent resistance to government to its ultimate extreme, out-Tolstoyed Tolstoy, out-Gandhied Gandhi, and practiced disarmament to the point of destroying all their weapons when they knew they were about to be attacked; a company anarchistic in principle, a quasi-hereditary theocracy in fact, with a leader whose followers believed him to be Christ yet publicly repudiated his authority, meanwhile obeying him implicitly and supporting him in luxury and vice while they lived in poverty and rectitude. That should be interesting. It is.

So says W. E. Garrison in reviewing *Slava Bohu, The Story of the Dukhobors,* by J. F. C. Wright,[48] a faithful account of this group of practical restorers of primitive Christianity.

[46]*Church Manual* (Boston: Publishers' agent, Trustees under the Will of Mary Baker Glover Eddy, 89th ed., 1940).

[47]C. Norton, *The Christian Science Church, Its Organization and Polity* (Boston: Christian Science Publishing Society, 1904), p. 31.

[48]Copyright 1941 Christian Century Foundation. Reprinted by permission from *The Christian Century* for January 22, 1941.

On December 12, 1896, three Tolstoyans published a pamphlet concerning the cruelties suffered by the Dukhobors in Caucasia. A letter of Tolstoy said that these simple and illiterate peasants had elected to live their lives in accord with the teachings of Jesus Christ and had actually accomplished that which other men only talked about. In 1934 a conclave under the direction of Peter Petrovich Verigin, the "divine" leader, said—

". . . We, the 'Named Dukhobors,' have been, are, and will be members of Christ's Church, confirmed by the Lord and Saviour Jesus Christ himself and assembled by the Apostles. . . ."

Verigin's letters are full of advice about how to reproduce the true life of primitive Christianity. The hectic history of the Dukhobor experiment is a faithful representation of the confusion and contradiction existing in the mind of Verigin as to just how the Christian life was and should be ordered. At one time he would advise his followers not to work but to beg their living so as to devote all time to preaching; again, he organized great industrial and manufacturing concerns which brought much profit to them—and to him. "Sometimes they seemed 'fools of God'; sometimes just plain fools."

Since their arrival in Canada in 1899 they have increased in number from less than 10,000 to some 17,000; but their unity of mind and purpose and organization has evaporated as their credulous faith in Verigin's divinity was dispelled by the heat of his violence and vice.

It is the perfect illustration of the decadence of a group which tried to be perfect in a sinful world, wanted to be in the world but not of it, could not make terms even with a government which was willing to do everything short of abdicating its functions in order to help them—a group which, with many virtues, had no sense.[49]

---

[49]*Ibid.*

Elmer T. Clark's little volume, *The Small Sects in America,* has a concluding chapter in which he summarizes "Characteristics of the Small Sects." He says:

The sects nearly all hark to the first century and believe it their duty to reproduce the primitive Church. . . . Such adaptations as are made are usually forced upon them over the bitter protests of many of their adherents, or ensue so gradually that the changes are unnoticed. . . . Many carry their conservatism to matters of nomenclature, and insist that "Bible things must be called by Bible names." A large number trace their ancestry back to Christ and the apostles, in plain defiance of history, and regard themselves as the "true church."[50]

This writer had occasion during 1942-45 to edit a survey entitled *Religion in Iowa,* in which thirty-two historians compiled the accounts of fifty-seven denominations in the Hawkeye state. These narratives and declarations of religious position show a living belief that certain modern denominations are truly the church of the first century. A. A. Jagnow of the American Lutheran Church says of the Augsburg Confession, "It set forth in bold outline the New Testament faith," and adds, "All churchly usages which are out of harmony with this fundamental New Testament faith are to be rejected." W. H. Blancke, writing for the United Lutheran Synod, said, "The Reformation did not mean a new church, but a return to the apostolic and early Church of Christ." Melvin Gingerich, Mennonite, traces his church to the Swiss Brethren of Ulrich Zwingli and Conrad Grebel, both of whom sought "a Christian church based upon the New Testament." This distinct effort on the part of the Mennonites to restore primitive Christianity has resulted in its breakdown into sixteen separate bodies in the United States, although they total less than a thousand congregations.[51] In the history of Mormonism, by Roy Cheville, it is clearly stated that this religion is "the Restoration" and alone possessed "the fulness of the Gospel." Ralph Bonkema reveals that the original name

[50]Copyright 1937 by Abingdon Press. Used by permission.
[51]*See* W. H. Lyon, *A Study of the Christian Sects* (Boston: Beacon Press, 1926), p. 86.

of the Christian Reformed Church early in its disassociation from the Reformed Church in America was "The True Dutch Reformed Church." Gerrit Vos says in his paper that Henry Danhof, the founder of his denomination, the Protestant Reformed Church, taught that God "hates the wicked every day even unto all eternity and from everlasting. It goes without saying that he [Danhof] based such teaching and testimony on the Word of God."

VI

From pre-Christian times the restoration principle has supplied the motive power of successful religious movements. In the Old Testament and among pagan faiths, as well as throughout the career of the Christian enterprise, we have seen in this chapter that zeal to recapture the faith of the Founder has given meaning and organized structure to the religious community.

Unfortunately for the peace and unity of religious faith, the understanding of *what* the Founder wanted to be kept fresh, to be made central in his way of living, has been as varied as the personalities of the restoration leaders themselves. From this long résumé of reformation idealism we see the life-giving power which comes to the individual or organization that feels itself completely "at one" with the purpose and fully identified with the actions of the Founder. Restoration movements get the same emotional results collectively that devotees of the ancient mysteries (or modern Holiness and healing cults, for that matter) gained for themselves individually. While this makes for power, it also induces a lack of appreciation for those not participating in and enjoying the benefits of the particular discoveries and experiences of the current movement. World-wide church unity suffers a handicap when restorationists conceive their own movement and practices as embracing practically all that is valid in religious living. The findings in the survey of this chapter are not on a unitive note. The world continues to wait for that rare combination in religion which may be the mark of true genius—*restoration* and *unity* as the twin goals of faith.

CHAPTER VII

An American Experiment
in Restorationism

The chief endeavor on the part of a modern communion of churches to employ the restoration principle in its religious theory and practice is seen in the case of the Christian Churches (Disciples of Christ). This body is the largest church of American origin, and is ninth in size among the Protestant communions.[1] The group had its origin during the opening decades of

---

[1] *The Year Book of American Churches, 1958,* listed the million-members-and-over churches (members 13 years of age or above) as follows:

Methodist	9,422,893
Southern Baptist	8,700,481
National Baptist Convention, U.S.A., Inc.	4,557,416
Protestant Episcopal (including infants)	2,852,965
Presbyterian Church in the U.S.A.	2,717,320
National Baptist Convention of America	2,668,799
United Lutheran Church in America	2,174,500
Lutheran Church, Missouri Synod	2,076,550
Disciples of Christ	1,922,484
Churches of Christ	1,700,000
Christ Unity Science Church	1,581,286
American Baptist Convention	1,528,210
Congregational and Christian	1,379,394
Mormons	1,289,581
African Methodist Episcopal	1,166,301

the nineteenth century on the frontier in what is now the Middle West when Thomas Campbell and his son Alexander joined forces with Barton W. Stone and Walter Scott to restore the principles of primitive Christianity. Its rapid rise to size among the religious bodies of the land makes a typically American success story. With no benefit of European cultural background or impetus from immigration this communion competed successfully with the power and prestige of Presbyterians, Methodists, Lutherans, Catholics, Baptists, and other Old World denominations. President James A. Garfield was one of its preachers. Today this fellowship embraces almost an even 2,000,000 members in the United States, with another 1,500,000 closely related members having separate census status under the name "Churches of Christ." These latter and more conservative restorers of primitive Christianity are to be found at their strongest in the southern states. The common property of these two bodies is loyalty to a "restoration plea," variously interpreted.

It is in the area of history that Disciples of Christ must be able to "give a reason for the faith that is in them." The chief apologetics for their existence and their distinctive form of the restoration plea in times past have issued from their theologians. From Thomas Campbell and his *Declaration and Address* (1809) onward, the validation of the proposal of Disciples of Christ has rested not upon the program itself, what it has done in the realm of events, and especially in creating church unity, but upon what its advocates would like to believe it could do.

The appeal to history for the validation of the restoration plea is not to fall prey to the psychology which claims that a thing is proven to be "true" when, for the moment, it works or gets results. At the same time, in the long run a program that is true to the divine Will—which can be known only in history—must prove itself able to operate and succeed in the only place where operation and success can have meaning—in the realm of human events. While a decade may not be decisive and a century guarantees no certainty, the multiples of decades and centuries must have a story to tell or we can be sure that no story, no truth, was given. The theologians may conjure up a great tale and sway our imagination, but it remains only a story until its principles become flesh and dwell among us as truly saving works. What necessarily begins as a theologian's apologetic is obliged to validate itself in life as the church historian's appeal to example.[2]

The Reformation of the Nineteenth Century, as Disciples have fondly denominated themselves, is old enough now to "get down to cases." The Bible informs us that Adam was 130 years old when his child, Seth, was born, "in his own likeness, after his image" (Genesis 5:3), thereby proving he could undertake with promise of success the program of subduing the earth and making it the footstool of God. Disciples of Christ are well past the 130-year mark, but are still like Adam in his earlier days when his only claim to fame was that his body had been divided.

I

Before enumerating such instances as are available to show how Disciples of Christ are contributing in a practical way to Christian unity today, we must trace briefly the form of forms that the restoration principle has taken among representative thinkers of this movement.

Thomas Campbell was the author of the charter document of Disciples of Christ, the *Declaration and Address,* published in 1809.[3] In recent decades there has been a strong tendency among historians and commentators on the program of this church to ascribe to the elder of the two reformers only the motive of desiring unity in the Christian world, without any particular program for reaching this grand objective. Indeed, the modern comment runs, Thomas Campbell was the irenic

---

[2]An excellent article by James B. Carr on "The Restoration Principle" in the January, 1953, *Manhattan Bible College News* is weak only at this point of historical validation. After noting the divisions over missionary societies and instrumental music, he says of the leaders, "They failed to use the principle, but the principle itself was valid." (p. 4.) While this may be true in part, in the final analysis a program is valid only as it affects helpfully the great majority of those it touches. In this instance the real question is, Does it create unity?

[3]The length of this chapter would be greatly extended if we should look into the work of the British predecessors who influenced Thomas and Alexander Campbell, and on the basis of which present-day members of the Disciple cause in Great Britain resent such a book title as W. E. Garrison's *An American Religious Movement* (St. Louis: Christian Board of Publication, 1945). For a single citation of such a leader, see the brief article by J. D. Phillips entitled "Archibald M'Lean, A Pre-Campbell 'Restorer'," in *The Truth,* July-August, 1947, pp. 147-149.

advocate of union, but his more dogmatic son Alexander displaced the author of the *Declaration,* and turned the movement into a crusade for a rigidly defined ecclesiastical order.

This is too simple an explanation of what transpired. A reading of the famous charter document makes it clear that Thomas Campbell thought he knew pretty well what he wanted in the matter of a restored, primitive, and, hence, a nearly perfect church. Early in the text of the proclamation he proposed to support:

A pure Gospel ministry, that shall reduce to practice that whole form of doctrine, worship, discipline, and government, expressly revealed and enjoined in the word of God.

If it be said that we should not expect fallible men in an evil world to achieve unity, the *Declaration* specifically meets this objection and admonishes us:

to conform to the model and adopt the practice of the primitive Church, expressly exhibited in the New Testament. . . . Were we, then, in our Church constitution and managements, to exhibit a complete conformity to the apostolic Church, would we not be, in that respect, as perfect as Christ intended we should be?

The next paragraph of the text again appeals to "the original pattern laid down in the New Testament." Several paragraphs later a sentence proposes to stand "upon clear and certain premises, and take up things just as the apostles left them."

When it is remembered that the Old Testament was the code book of a religious institution with visible unity in its priesthood, liturgy, and rules for living, Mr. Campbell is expressing himself clearly when he says:

The New Testament is as perfect a constitution for the worship, discipline, and government of the New Testament Church, and as perfect a rule for the particular duties of its members, as the Old Testament was for the worship, discipline, and government of the Old Testament Church, and the particular duties of its members.

137

The Postscript published three months after the *Declaration* declares that it is the intention of its advocates to provide soon a "Christian Catechism" containing

a catechetical exhibition of the fulness and precision of the Holy Scriptures upon the entire subject of Christianity—an exhibition of that complete system of faith and duty expressly contained in the Sacred Oracles, respecting the doctrine, worship, discipline and government of the church.

In the light of the extracts given above it is apparent that, for a time, there moved in the mind of Thomas Campbell the idea that there was a long lost but simple solution for the ills of a divided Christendom. This remedy was the redefinition of Christianity in New Testament terms, embracing doctrine, worship, discipline, and government.

Thomas Campbell never wrote his "catechetical exhibition." Why? Either he could not or he would not set forth the Christian religion as largely an unchanging set of doctrines, forms, and practices. He lived the rest of his life as an advocate of great Christian principles, but he never returned to ecclesiastical definitions.

This fact is an almost lost parable of the history of Disciples of Christ. In delineating the restoration plea, Thomas Campbell never wrote or spoke on the theme in any major article or sermon, but simply lived a good, Christian life after the publication of the *Declaration and Address*. Perhaps such small efforts as he did make in the direction of a definition showed him the dangers and difficulties of the task, e.g., his test question for those wanting to become charter members of the first church he organized at Brush Run in 1811. There he manufactured a brief human creed which was so obviously unsatisfactory and unapostolic that it was promptly abandoned.

Thomas Campbell's heart and instinct were superior to his theory of constitutional ecclesiastical law. This is not surprising to us today when we remember that his generation was bound by certain preconceptions about the nature of the Bible which no longer generally prevail. As F. D. Kershner said, "Christian

138

unity is not as easy a proposition as it appeared to Thomas Campbell."[4] Our judgment as to why this is true is that the program of the *Declaration* is Bible-centered rather than focused on loyalty to Jesus Christ. To quote the original document:

With you all we desire to unite in the bonds of an entire Christian unity—Christ alone being the *head*, the center, *his word the rule;* an explicit belief of, and manifest *conformity to it* in all things—*the terms.*[5]

It is one of the insights of devoted biblical scholarship since Thomas Campbell's time to see that loyalty to Jesus Christ takes precedence over and gives meaning to a Christian use of the New Testament. The New Testament is itself the record of a fellowship created by loyalty to the accepted Messiah and Savior, a fellowship which transcended differences of worship methods and ethical interests, so long as an increasing embodiment of the will of Christ was ever the goal of the companions in the Way. Peter's and Paul's almost violent divergence on the race problem, John's unique and (as far as the record goes) unshared interest in the theology of pre-existence, the concentration of the author of the Pastoral Epistles on the imminence of Jesus' bodily return to earth—these are examples in a panorama of interests which leads to modern books having such titles as *The Varieties of New Testament Religion.*[6] Increasingly it is becoming apparent to sincere Christians seeking unity that Thomas Campbell's insight in his later years was profound. He could not reduce the New Testament to a catechism, but he could find a true unity with all who wanted to grow in the Christian life on the basis of the New Testament revelation of the will of Christ. His spiritual descendants in convention assembled in Denver, Colorado, in 1938 found no difficulty or incongruity in taking fellowship in the World Council of Churches, which has as its creed the words "Jesus is God." Loyalty to Jesus increasingly became the key to the elder Campbell's faith.

---

[4]From *The Christian Union Overture,* p. 30. Copyright 1923 by Bethany Press. Used by permission.
[5]Italics added.
[6]By E. F. Scott.

While Thomas Campbell did not bring forth a specific definition of the plea, he did something of much greater importance when he explored the method by which any truth may be expected to be found. Late in the text of the *Declaration* he said, "It is not the voice of the multitude, but the voice of truth, that has power with the conscience, that can produce rational conviction and acceptable obedience."

The six pages of comment on this section of the document of 1809 by F. D. Kershner is one of the most important, and one of the most neglected, examples of Disciple philosophy in existence. A few excerpts will reveal the nature and direction of Mr. Campbell's thought. Dr. Kershner says:

Thomas Campbell . . . appeals from the ecclesiastical decisions of popes and cardinals to what he considers the more certain infallibility of the common mind as the latter is found embodied in the Christian thought of the church membership as a whole. . . . The only test of truth is its universal acceptance by right thinking people everywhere. . . . The common mind, the universal reason, is not always incarnate in the prejudiced and turbulent mass of humanity. It is, however, always present in the thoughtful consensus of the majority of intelligent, candid, and honest seekers after truth.[7]

There is brilliant insight in this conception of the path to agreement in the essentials of Christian work and worship. Mr. Campbell glimpsed it in some measure and sketched its outlines hazily. It remains for his spiritual children to explore further the truths that may be found as the common mind of the world-wide church discloses what is vital and what is merely curious and local in expressing the program of Christianity. We shall return to this theme at the conclusion of the present chapter.

II

Alexander Campbell never defined his conception of the restoration plea. We shall note later that he and other pioneers made approaches in this direction by describing certain elements

---

[7] *Op. cit.*, p. 101.

of the New Testament church—but the fact remains that the number-one leader of Disciples of Christ nowhere set down in order a catalog of the "express terms and approved precedents" of church organization and life in the Bible which they assumed were there.

It is fortunate for Disciples of Christ today that this is true, for many reasons. One is the plain fact, more and more clearly delineated by the historians, that it may be said there were two Alexander Campbells. His latest biographer, Benjamin Smith, so states the matter. A graduate thesis at Phillips University by Evelyn Dubbs entitled *Alexander Campbell in the Christian Baptist and Millennial Harbinger,* written in 1942, traces the differences between the iconoclastic reformer of the 1820's and the more sober and constructive editor of the *Millennial Harbinger.*[8] In 1823 he inveighed against Bible societies, missionary societies, and educational societies; some years later he aided and encouraged all these and more. In the *Millennial Harbinger* for 1851 (p. 581) he said that the use of an organ in church "would be as a cowbell in a concert." The anti-organ Churches of Christ today love to quote the young Mr. Campbell; Disciples of Christ prefer to cite the later Mr. Campbell; but for neither of the two groups, incipient in the movement from the start, did he define the restoration plea.

One might assume that *The Christian System,* published in 1836, would include such a delineation. It appeared that the making of a definition was in his mind when he said on page 74:

The Christian institution has its facts, its precepts, its promises, its ordinances, and their meaning or doctrine. These are not matters of policy, of arrangement, of expediency, but of divine and immutable ordination and continuance. Hence the faith, the worship, and the righteousness; or the doctrine, the piety, and the

[8]It is possible to observe the two tendencies in the work of Mr. Campbell and yet not be subject to the "common fallacy" of distinguishing "two Campbells," as the well-informed biographer and scintillating writer, Eva Jean Wrather, puts the matter. Miss Wrather is right in confuting any schizophrenic division in the mind of so balanced a person, and in making the point, otherwise overlooked, that there are as timeless and balanced utterances on Christian unity principles in the *Christian Baptist* as there are in the *Millennial Harbinger.* See, for example, the Campbell letter in the *Christian Baptist* "To an Independent Baptist." Eva Jean Wrather, *Alexander Campbell and His Relevance for Today* (Nashville: Disciples of Christ Historical Society, 1953), p. 8.

morality of the gospel institution are not legitimate subjects of human legislation, alteration, or arrangement. No man nor community can touch these and be innocent. These rest upon the wisdom and authority of Jehovah.

But Mr. Campbell was too well acquainted with the history of reformation to expect a definition formulated in the nineteenth century to supersede all others. The direction of his thinking is more apparent on page 121:

The grandeur, sublimity and beauty of the foundation of hope, and of ecclesiastical or social union, established by the author and founder of Christianity, consisted in this,—that THE BELIEF OF ONE FACT *and that upon the best evidence in the world, is all that is requisite, as far as faith goes, to salvation. The belief of this* ONE FACT, *and submission to* ONE INSTITUTION *expressive of it, is all that is required of Heaven to admission into the church.* . . .The one fact is expressed in a single proposition—*that Jesus the Nazarene is the Messiah.* . . . The *one institution* is baptism.

Here was a program presented in 1836 which embraced his youthful perception of the only hopeful way to union when he said in 1810:

"We have decided, therefore, to lift it [the New Testament] up as a standard for the Church, to open the gates of admission into the Church as wide as the gates of heaven."[9]

The significance of Mr. Campbell's thinking about his program for restoration, as compared with the scores of other efforts in this field, has been carefully assessed by Dr. W. E. Garrison on pages 39-40 of *Religion Follows the Frontier.* Just now it is our purpose only to note that the sober judgment of the sage of Bethany usually was inclusive rather than exclusive in his thought of the Christian community.[10] For this reason he defined

[9]Robert Richardson, *Memoirs of Alexander Campbell* (Philadelphia: Lippincott, 1868-70), I, 341.
[10]*Millennial Harbinger,* September, 1837.

the restoration plea only in broad terms. His statement in his Lunenberg Letter of 1837 is representative:

But who is a Christian? I answer, Every one that believes in his heart that Jesus of Nazareth is the Messiah, the Son of God; repents of his sins, and obeys him in all things according to his measure of knowledge of his will.[11]

III

Walter Scott, the flaming evangelist of Disciples on the Western Reserve, did not fully agree with Alexander Campbell on the subject of the restoration plea. In the same year that the *Christian System* appeared from the pen of Campbell, 1836, Scott issued a volume entitled *The Gospel Restored*. In the preface he said:

In 1823 a plea for a particular ecclesiastical order was put forth publicly, by Brother Alexander Campbell. This for distinction's sake was called the ancient order. . . . Presiding at that time, over a church which had already attained the ancient order, or at least as much of it as seems even now to be attained, the gospel, or rather a uniform authoritative plan of preaching it, became more the object of my attention. . . . In 1827 the True Gospel was restored.

Why 1827? Because on November 18 of that year Scott baptized William Amend who Baxter, Scott's early biographer, says was "beyond all question, the first person in modern times who received the ordinance of baptism in perfect accordance with apostolic teaching and usage."[12]

---

[11]In momentary controversy this was not always the case. He excluded the New England Unitarian Congregationalists from his followers in 1846. They proposed union on profession of Christian character. He retreated to an incipient theological base, writing, "I cannot imagine a more radical mistake than to substitute, at the very threshold of an overture for Christian union, a declaration of our faith in what constitutes a Christian for a declaration of our faith in Jesus Christ himself. A union founded upon a definition of a Christian, rather than upon a definition of Jesus Christ himself!!" For his full statement of this particular case see the *Millennial Harbinger*, 1846, pp. 216-225, 388-394, 450-454, 634-638, 686-695.

[12]William Baxter, *Life of Elder Walter Scott* (Cincinnati: Bosworth, Chase and Hall, 1874), p. 108.

Scott had previously referred to this claim of priority or originality more or less subtly in the May 7, 1832, issue of his journal, the *Evangelist*.[13] There he said:

A few years ago the great desideratum with Reformers was—

The bond entire of Christian Union

. . . to present the whole in actual practice for the inspection, adoption and benefit of men, was the consummation to be wished.

This has been done; the entire First-Principle scheme was, a few years since, put into operation, and then, *for the first time,* disciples were let upon the divine institution on the plan of the Ancient Gospel and Ancient Order combined. . . .[14]

Walter Scott seems not to have been interested in defining the government and works (such as missions, music, and the other outward items on which Disciples of Christ have divided) of the New Testament church. He was interested in its doctrine and ordinances. In the fourth issue of his magazine, April 2, 1832, he introduced a series of articles on the steps of salvation with this statement:

For reasons which it is allowed the reader to infer, I am anxious the EVANGELIST should embody a just and scriptural definition of Faith; not because I conceive it probable my readers have not already read and thought of this important principle in the Ancient Gospel; but generally, if not universally, our attempts to define faith, have not, I think, been very eminently characterized for that sobriety of mind which willingly contents itself with what the Scriptures have said on the subject. At the restoration of the Ancient Gospel, the first point to be gained was to arrange the several items of Faith—repentance, baptism, remission of sins, the holy spirit, and the resurrection. A second and distinct effort called on us to supply the auditors with definitions, so that the proclamation of the Ancient Gospel was distinguished 1st, for the arrangement of its terms, and 2nd for orderly and Scriptural definitions of these terms, beginning with Faith.

---

[13]The book, *The Gospel Restored,* was issued as the equivalent of the twelve issues of the *Evangelist* for 1836, and was sent to the subscribers to that magazine in their stead. Earlier references than the claim made in the book of 1836 are to be found in various issues of the *Evangelist* antedating the book.

[14]Italics added.

Then followed the article defining Faith.

A reading of the remaining copies of the *Evangelist* brings one to observe that Mr. Scott thought little of defining or making a comprehensive exposition of the restoration plea. A series of articles on "Reformation" ran over a period of years. All of them were pointed in the direction of seeing Christianity as a means to good character. Another series on "Church Order" took up several phases of the church's life, with what we may call descriptions of the plea's practical workings. They derived from the growing need to obtain co-operation in evangelism and other general duties of the churches. Like Mr. Campbell, Scott used several articles in the 1830's to explain that human slavery had no significance for Christianity. The restoration plea of Disciples of Christ involved character but Christian character had no reference to keeping human beings in perpetual slavery.

The single point of Scott's message to the Christian world was reiterated many, many times. His book, *The Gospel Restored,* affirms the discovery of the Messiahship of Jesus as the grounds on which "all were freely and lovingly admitted to the rights and privileges of the Christian church." He added:

The late restoration of the gospel was in nothing more singular than in its proposing again this faith in all its pristine singleness and simplicity.[15]

Scott repeated this message in *The Messiahship* published in 1859.

A measure of irritation and disagreement came to exist between Alexander Campbell and Walter Scott because of the latter's oft-repeated claim to having first proclaimed the true gospel (the full name of his journal was *The Evangelist of the True Gospel*). A résumé of this disagreement is to be found in the December, 1838, *Evangelist.* The new and different element in Scott's understanding of Christianity was the matter of immediate acceptance of the offer of salvation, and immediate remission of sins in the promptly subsequent baptism.

---

[15]*Evangelist,* November 1, 1838.

Scott believed that his newly discovered truth about Christianity would quickly engulf the denominations. He wrote a tract of some size on *The Union of Christians* about 1850 in which he said:

The opponent objects again, "Your scheme will only create another sect." Grant it. But then it will be a sect which, in its progress, will consume all others. As Moses's rod ate up the rods of the magicians, the true Creed will destroy all others, and the true principles of union consume all those of mere party origin. Reformers, having hitherto failed to select and appreciate the constitutional truth of the Christian system, their labors became schismatic, and they themselves the founders of sects. The aims and destinies of the holders of the true faith are higher. The mission is Union—the annihilation of sects and parties, and the recovery of the church.

It is a major handicap to Disciples of Christ as effective advocates of restorationism that their two most prominent early leaders did not fully agree in their analysis or definition of the restoration principle. In the *Millennial Harbinger,* October, 1838, Campbell wrote an article entitled "Events of 1823 and 1827" in which he protested against Scott's "invidious style of fixing dates, places, and persons . . . for the restoration of the ancient gospel." He said, "I am thankful that I never put the title 'Christianity Restored' nor 'Gospel Restored' to any thing I ever wrote." However, he conceded,

although I [still] cannot regard any thing done by him in 1827, or myself in 1823, as a restoration of the gospel of Christ either to the church or to the world, I do consider that he practically carried out the principles of reformation as before understood . . . in the *Christian Baptist* and in my debate with M'Calla . . . more fully and effectually, as well as more successfully, than before attempted or accomplished by any one. . . .[16]

IV

E. E. Snoddy has a fine paragraph in praise of Barton W. Stone which credits him with many priorities in the development

---

[16]*Millennial Harbinger,* 1840, p. 188.

of Disciples—but the list says nothing about a definition of the restoration plea. This is not because of a lack of materials from Stone's pen. He was accepted as the theologian of the group which organized and then disbanded the Springfield Presbytery. After the publication of the *Apology* of the Springfield body in 1804, Stone set forth a theological statement of thirty-six pages in 1805. His biographer discounts the resulting storm of criticism of the document by saying, "Heirs of the Stone movement have not taken seriously this early theology of Stone.[17]

If Stone and Campbell had attempted to define the restoration concept about 1830, the time when union overtures between their followers were becoming promising, it seems certain that their resulting documents would have varied considerably. The Bethany scholar was not happy about the claim of the Kentucky Christians, gathered by Stone in a successful brotherhood of churches before Alexander Campbell came to America in 1809, that they had been proclaiming the basic ideals of the two movements three times as long as the Eastern brethren. Campbell accused the Western Christians of " 'sectarian peculiarities' " but hoped they would overcome them as they were " 'fast advancing in [his view of] the Christian Scripture.' "[18] The *Millennial Harbinger* did little to promote the union, but Stone's *Christian Messenger* did much for the cause.[19]

Stone had controversies in print with the Campbells, for example, on the Atonement, in 1833. A more important difference, for it concerned the name of the movement and was thus closer to the "essentials" in which there should be unity, found Alexander Campbell standing alone against his father, Stone, and Scott.[20] Characteristically enough, he persisted with a great weight of words and fastened upon the movement the name it long has borne in the United States Census—"Disciples of Christ"—probably to the distaste of most of the humble followers in the churches then and now.

---

[17]From *Barton Warren Stone,* by C. C. Ware, p. 152. Copyright 1932 by Bethany Press. Used by permission.

[18]*Ibid.,* 227-228.

[19]*Ibid.,* p. 249.

[20]*Ibid.,* pp. 310f.

Definitions of Christian faith in exact but human terms were foreign to the nature of Barton W. Stone. He thought not enough of his own importance to be a great man in his day of controversy. He wrote, "The great secret of church government and organization has been almost overlooked. It is the indwelling of the Holy Spirit in each believer and member of the church.[21]

Specifically an item of the restoration plea is the matter of the ordination of the ministry. On this subject Stone differed radically from all other major early leaders. Today, North Carolina is the only state where the substance of the Stone tradition prevails in this field. Briefly stated by one of his congregations, the practice is as follows:

. . . as we have no account in the New Testament of ordination to the ministry done by the church alone, or by the church in conjunction with the eldership, but that as we have particular accounts of its being done by the eldership or presbytery, therefore the eldership alone with the recommendation of the church, had the authority to ordain, when they concurred with the church in regard to the qualifications of the person to be ordained.[22]

To summarize the experience of the "big four" early leaders of Disciples of Christ in their approach to a definition of the restoration plea, we may take the judgment of Principal William Robinson, founder of Overdale College, Selly Oak, Birmingham, England:

For them Christianity was conditioned by loyalty to and trust in, a Person, rather than by obedience to legal codes and intellectual assent to dogmas. In the course of their work, however—which was necessarily work of a somewhat polemical character—they were driven to assert that the way to unity was by "restoring the New Testament pattern of the Church." It was an unquestioned assumption amongst Protestants of their day (Canon Streeter and his predecessors in the field not having lived) that such a pattern did exist. . . . Unfortunately we have been haunted by the idea

---

[21]*Christian Messenger,* Vol. 14, p. 119.
[22]*Ibid.,* Vol. I, p. 139.

that there is a codified pattern of the ideal church within the pages of the New Testament.[23]

V

The later history of Disciples of Christ has been much like the experience of the first-generation leaders—their theological stock in trade has been the assumption that the Bible contains the exact description of a once-and-forever-delivered, or defined, church in organization, work, and worship. As the *Christian Standard* put it, "The very essence of our plea is that the church, *in its every detail,* must be scriptural, must conform to the New Testament model." A recent preachment states the case simply, referring to the New Testament period:

In all the places where the church was found uniformity obtained in all things essential. All had the same creed, all accepted the sacred names. They observed the ordinances alike. The organizations were alike and in every church there was the one uniform plan of admittance.

In the above we see uniformity. Here is a perfect pattern.[24]

But, having asserted the claim, no one among Disciples of Christ has ever gone on to perform what ought to be a comparatively simple operation, namely, to set down in some order (so that the wayfaring seeker, though a fool, might understand) the substance of this program.

The experience of Disciples of Christ as a separate communion of churches has been closely parallel to that of Protestantism as a whole in this regard. To make a very long story short, it may be said that when, in search of freedom, the long-fermenting Reformation of the sixteenth century came to pass, an organizing principle was needed to provide unity and structure for the movement. The proposed solution of this problem was the proclamation of the grand assumption of creedal Protestantism that the Bible contains an articulated, consistent, and self-

[23]Published first in *The Student Movement* magazine, England; quoted in the *Christian Quarterly*, England, April 1924, p. 37.
[24]From *The New Testament Church Pattern*, by P. H. Welshimer, p. 8.

authenticating system of doctrine that would become increasingly evident to any reader and student of ordinary intelligence. Upon this assumption there was reared, time after time, a specific creedal summary of the faith, each one gathering into its borders of fellowship such people as admired the particular bill of goods described on the given doctrinal wrapper. The failure of each new device to do its stipulated task—to define the faith so clearly that all reasonable men would confess the truth—was overlooked by the devotees of each new and shining instrument of Christian theological exposition, so enamoured were they of the work of their hands. Thus the record of Protestantism has been a succession of schisms, a procession of failures in the professed search for a scriptural fellowship. Only in modern times has Protestantism stopped to ask itself the searching question, Will creedal, ironclad (but human) definitions do the job of creating a world-wide Christian fellowship?

Likewise the restoration movement, in search of liberation from the historic fragmentation of Christian fellowship, with prophetic vision glimpsed a new basis of fraternity with "the gates for admission into the church as wide as the gates of heaven," as Alexander Campbell put it. But when it came to setting down the terms of this new association, and to outlining its organization, Disciples of Christ fell under the spell of the same theological safeguard of unity that had tempted so many previous Protestant movements. Avoiding the formation of a simple document of creed, due to the lack of a central organization in the new group and because of an early tradition against creeds on principle, individual leaders began to hedge the restoration fellowship with particular demands. Mr. Campbell changed his mind about the necessity of immersion baptism, and fastened his changed position upon the congregations, contrary to the disposition of Stone.[25] What began as a free fellowship of Christian seekers after biblical guidance before long became a more or less rigidly described group of those who had

[25] In the overtures leading to the union of Campbell and Stone forces in 1832, the latter wrote that one of Campbell's objections to the merger was that the Stone Christians "have fellowship and communion with unimmersed persons" (Ware, *op. cit.*, p. 229). In a "retrospect" by Stone in 1833 he reported that he had frequently preached on "Four Different Kinds of Union," Number 3 being "Water Union, based on immersion, an unstable compact" (Ware, *ibid.*, p. 258).

found "the truth" about organization, work, and worship. Protestantism then discovered that it had gained another fragment, much akin to the others. The incontestable denouement of its claim to be a perfect union movement came with its own unhappy split into two bodies in 1906, when the "Churches of Christ" emerged, and another withdrawal of independent brethren into a "Church of Christ Number Two" in 1955, with its own yearbook, list of preachers, and roster of missionary agencies.

In other words, while the early leaders of Disciples of Christ never defined the restoration plea exactly, they did not hesitate to do the next thing to definition, and that was to describe it. The history of this process of description is too long to be included here, but is summarized in a quotation later in this chapter. The conscious or unconscious wisdom of Disciples of Christ in offering partial and unofficial suggestions toward description, rather than exact definition, was observed by I. N. McCash as follows:

Since Christianity itself is not defined; but described, qualities named, commands given, precepts stated, etc., we get a concept when these are put together as a mosaic of Christianity.

The nearest definition of pure religion is the epistle of James 1:27. However that describes what a man with pure religion will do; namely, show benevolence toward others and purity toward self. If God in the soul of men, binding them together, is religion, James tells how it expresses itself. A definition must include everything of the kind and exclude everything not of the kind defined.[26]

VI

A particular demonstration of the loss of the fraternal concept integral to the early aims of Mr. Campbell's restoration idealism is to be seen in the career of the Churches of Christ, marked by that official name in the United States Census of Religious Bodies to distinguish them from Disciples of Christ. These two bodies were one until 1906. When the government census of churches was being compiled in that year, its bureau

---

[26]Letter of Dr. McCash to this writer, November 11, 1944.

offices received requests from conservative members of the restoration movement asking that they not be counted a part of the group as it was then described. In accordance with this desire appropriate census-taking forms were sent to J. W. Shepherd, Nashville, Tennessee, and the United States Census Bureau gave him the necessary assistance which enabled him to survey and report the constituency of the dissenting group. The numbers reported in that and subsequent United States censuses were:

	Churches	Members
1906	2,649	159,658
1916	5,570	317,937
1926	6,226	433,714
1936	3,815	309,551

The difference between Disciples of Christ and the Churches of Christ derives from the diverse interests which characterized the restoration movement in its formative years. As is shown in a previous volume by this writer,[27] many streams of particular religious concern flowed together to make their fellowship. Conceived in the love of the simple Bible account of original Christianity and opposed especially to the narrow and creedalized denominations then existing, the movement was nourished into notable proportions during the second great awakening of the early nineteenth century. Concerned first with their freedom, as soon as they stopped to consider a positive apology for their separate existence, they transmuted their negative reaction against formal creeds into an affirmative assumption that the New Testament writers had described precisely what the age-long, continuing church should be in organization, worship, and life. To repeat a quotation from Thomas Campbell already used in this chapter:

The New Testament is as perfect a constitution for the worship, discipline, and government of the New Testament Church, and as perfect a rule for the particular duties of its members, as the Old Testament was for the worship, discipline, and government

---

[27] *The Grounds of Divisions Among the Disciples of Christ* (Chicago: privately printed, 1940), especially Chapter III.

of the Old Testament Church, and the particular duties of its members.

Thus there came to be, very early in the career of this movement, interest not only in (1) Christian unity in a new freedom, but also (2) a return to the doctrine, ordinances, and discipline of the New Testament church.[28]

Broadly speaking, it may be said that number 1 above generated the present fellowship called Disciples of Christ, and that number 2 gave rise to the Churches of Christ. If we should use the classification made by Troeltsch in his *Social Teaching of the Christian Churches,* Disciples would be among the "church" type and the Churches of Christ among the "sect" type. By "church" is meant that body of conceptions which Principal William Robinson could represent in his pamphlet, *New Testament Christianity*[29] by saying, "From the beginning they have been 'high churchmen' . . . " because they "never ceased to stress the visible and corporate character of the Church as the Divine Society," and rejected "legalized methods and structural forms which are a contradiction of the *living* nature of the Church." By "sect" is meant those worshipers whose aim is absolute ritualistic and doctrinal correctness regardless of whether the program actually succeeds in gaining a favorable and general response of the human race. The correctness of this depiction is to be seen by reading the periodical literature of the Churches of Christ. It includes such characterizing names as the *Truth, Truth in Love, Truth Advance, Primitive Gospel Herald, Gospel Guardian, Lord's Way, Old Paths Advocate, Sound Words,* and the *Macedonian Call.*

No unsuspecting Christian who might come upon these journals and read them would imagine that they were the heralds of a unity movement. Interests of primary concern in some of

---

[28]This analysis of the career of the total movement is confirmed by A. W. Fortune, who says, "The controversies through which the Disciples have passed from the beginning to the present time have been the result of two different interpretations of their mission. There have been those who believed it is the spirit of the New Testament Church that should be restored, and in our method of working the church must adapt itself to changing conditions. There have been those who regarded the New Testament Church as a fixed pattern for all time, and our business is to hold rigidly to that pattern regardless of consequences. Because of these two attitudes conflicts were inevitable." *The Disciples in Kentucky* (Convention of the Christian Churches in Kentucky, 1932), p. 383.

[29](Birmingham, England: Berean Press, n. d.), p. 6.

these papers are the claim that only those persons using the physical ritual of these congregations in baptism are Christians, that there is really no worship achieved unless certain ecclesiastical implements are employed in the ordinance of fellowship, that the totality of the worship service is invalid unless it follows a prescribed and unvarying form, that those who associate themselves in missionary societies are apostates from Christianity, and that the use in church of a piano or an organ is sinful.

It is scarcely necessary to add that, this being the attitude of the Churches of Christ, no group in the religious world other than themselves considers them to be a unity movement. Their program for reunion is as rigid and uncompromising as that of the Roman Catholic church. For good or for ill, it is a fact that many members of the brotherhood of Disciples of Christ today do not know that the Churches of Christ were once a part of their own family. It is true that some members of the two bodies are deeply concerned about their separation and, starting in 1943, published occasionally a *Christian Unity Quarterly*. The few unity conferences of these groups, which began at Detroit in 1938, were poorly attended, were heavily attacked by the journals of the Churches of Christ, were largely ignored by those of Disciples, and were soon abandoned. This writer deplores but recognizes these facts. The statistics reported for the United States Census above reflect a distinct process of fragmentation going on among the Churches of Christ, meaning that many congregations do not want to be counted with the others, or they adhere to the Old Testament doctrine by which they simply do not want to be counted. Their ministers refuse to have fellowship in the loosely knit and quite unofficial ministerial associations common to the towns and cities of the United States. Their missionaries abroad avoid friendly fellowship with other Christian missionaries in their areas—not because many of them do not crave to have it, but for fear of what they know a report of their action would mean to their support from the denomination. The few fraternally minded leaders among them who want at least to attend and observe the proceedings of such bodies as the World Council of Churches do so only with the fear that their fellow Christians at home will hear of it and read them out of the fellowship. It is for these reasons that no responsible judge today looks upon the Churches of Christ as a unity movement.

A confirmation of the foregoing judgments is given by L. L. Brigance, who published a series of writings in a weekly journal, the *Gospel Advocate,* under the heading "Studies in the Restoration." They were extensive enough to require space two or more times per month from the middle of 1939 into 1942. With excellent skill and admirable fairness of statement Mr. Brigance analyzes this writer's volume, published in 1940, *The Grounds of Divisions Among the Disciples of Christ.* He then does a thing never before specifically attempted, that is, he accepts the challenge to list precisely the marks of identification of a Church of Christ according to his "Restoration Plea." They are:

1. The Names and Descriptive Titles of the Church and its Members
2. Organization, or Church Government
   ". . . the saints, or members in general, the bishops, or elders; and the deacons. . . . Any organization other than this is unauthorized in the Scriptures."
3. Doctrine
   "The doctrine taught by the early church . . . is the New Testament."
4. Work
   Development of its own members, benevolence, and the preaching of the Gospel.
5. Worship[30]

The fact that there are frequent schisms among the Churches of Christ involving all of these items was not discussed by their author. Their utter futility as a basis of unity is seen in one break in the fellowship over proposition number 4, which was so complete that in 1925 the dissenting group brought out its own separate *Year Book Containing List of Preachers of Churches of*

[30]*Gospel Advocate,* January 2, 1941. All quotations from *Gospel Advocate* are used by permission.

Christ, with 150 names. The same result could be cited on each of the other items.

Succeeding articles proceeded to elaborate the meaning of these five characteristics. For example, a true church, said Mr. Brigance, abhors co-operation.

The first symptoms of unrest and dissatisfaction and a desire for change began to appear about 1830 in "cooperation meetings." Sometimes a few individuals would organize with president, secretary, and treasurer, raise means by contributions, and employ preachers to go into destitute places. This was called "individual cooperation." Then a few churches would unite for this purpose, and the organization was known as the "cooperation of churches." The next step was the organization of the churches of a county, which was later enlarged to include churches of the counties composing a congressional district and called "district meetings." In June, 1835 [sic] a meeting for the entire state of Indiana was held in Indianapolis. This became an annual affair. The next step was the national organization known as the American Christian Missionary Society in 1849.[31]

Again, the use of settled pastors is pointed out as a mark of infidelity.

The unhappy portion of Mr. Brigance's long exposition is where he feels obliged to examine his own household. After 151 years of effort under the most favorable conditions ever given in history, his program has won a following optimistically but quite uncritically estimated at something less than one per cent of the nation. But even in this select circle there are ominous signs of churches and preachers falling away from the infallible formula for bringing in the kingdom. "Have they remained true to their strict adherence to the word of God? Do they still oppose both in theory and practice every innovation upon the ancient order, or have they weakened here and there? . . . there are evidences of trends in that direction."[32] Specifically:

One of the greatest evils among the churches of Christ today is the professional preacher—the "modern pastor." His growth has

[31]*Ibid.,* Febuary 20, 1941.
[32]*Ibid.,* May 22, 1941.

been rapid. Twenty-five years ago he was scarcely in existence. Today he is among us on every hand.[33]

In the third place, instrumental music voids the validity of any worship in which it is used. Mr. Brigance said, "organized effort and instrumental music, these two, but the greatest of these is instrumental music. It has been our observation and experience that the organ has caused more strife, bitterness, and division than any other single thing."[34] The reason for not using organs in worship is because the early Christians did not use instruments, and any such act lacking in primitive worship is a positive command not to do so today. To quote Mr. Brigance:

God gave the world a perfect system of religion at the beginning of the Christian age, and it cannot be improved. It is fixed and permanent. It is inflexible. It is perfectly adapted to the needs of humanity in every age. To modify it is to impeach the wisdom of God and to usurp his authority. It is the sin of presumption.[35]

Or, as stated in another article, "The little end of the tap-root of the division in the ranks of the Restoration Movement is not instruments of music and human societies, but a lack of respect for the authority of God's word."[36]

The basic assumption in the argument against instrumental music is of a most curious nature. It goes as follows: God approved of instrumental music in the "inferior" worship of Old Testament times, as the Bible records about the temple service indicate. However, when God decided to send Jesus and give a New Testament, he arranged to test the insight and the devout attention to details of revelation not by specifically giving a command *not* to use instruments of music after the year A.D. 30 (that would have been too easy), but by simply *not saying* anything about the subject. Thus he would see if his followers in the new era would note that by maintaining silence on the

[33]*Ibid.*, December 4, 1941.
[34]*Ibid.*, March 27, 1941.
[35]*Ibid.*
[36]*Ibid.*, Febuary 6, 1941.

topic it should be apparent to any truly devout Christian that the instruments, formerly approved, were now banned. This "argument from silence" is at the foundation of Church of Christ doctrine.

Fourth, says Mr. Brigance, true Christianity is marked by a refusal to have anything to do with the denominations. "None who have not been immersed are Christians. To recognize them as such is to deceive them and to take liberties with the word of God that neither man nor angel has a right to do." Thus "to cooperate with them in their religious activities, to call on them to 'lead in prayer,' to exchange pulpits with their preachers, to join their ministerial associations, etc. is either to recognize them as Christians or to deceive them."[37]

Ernest Beam of Los Angeles, a Church of Christ minister, brought out in 1949 a booklet of thirty-two pages ("Beam-Brewer" The Study That Was To Have Been) describing the "eight disfellowshipping movements" then subdividing these churches. In 1955 Yater Tant and E. R. Harper, both Church of Christ leaders, debated each other in Lufkin, Texas, each accusing the other of unscripturalness (meaning infidelity). This, then, is the condition and status of that segment of the restoration movement claiming to be its only pure expression. What we have written above is from one of its mildest journals. If one prefers his religion with a strong dash of tabasco, he should read the Bible Banner, succeeded by the Gospel Guardian, papers with no mean circulation or editorial capacity. The October, 1944, issue of the Banner makes its contribution to world peace and Christian unity by proclaiming that "the Baptist church exists and functions for the exclusive purpose of keeping souls from reaching Christ."[38] Statements in the same temper, and referring not only to the denominations but also to large sections of the Churches of Christ could be multiplied.

The latest serious effort to solve the problem of divisions in the Churches of Christ is the book, We Be Brethren, by J. D. Thomas, a professor at Abilene Christian College and Director

[37]Ibid., April 17, 1941.
[38]p. 11.

158

of the Annual Lectureship at Abilene which draws thousands of elders and ministers to its program. He recognizes the seriousness of schism in his fellowship. One commentator said, ". . . we have ceased to be a united effort to bring unity to the Christian world and now espouse the cause of religious division in the name of Biblical truth."[39]

Dr. Thomas offers a "Standard Diagram of Authority" and a " 'Pattern Principle' for Examples" to enable Christians to know which New Testament examples are binding and which are not. He insists that continued division is not primarily a problem of uncharitable persons when he says, "but in the final analysis there has been confusion about how to discern God's *pattern* revelation." He seeks "a correct knowledge of God's pattern will," saying that churches should "not be distracted by personalities or minor matters until we know *exactly* what God wants us to know."[40] Throughout the book the assumption is made that the New Testament is the vehicle or container of a pattern of church specifications.

This search for hidden patterns results in a caricature of the revealing God. Everywhere it is assumed that revelation is complete and adequate, but has been fragmentary, piecemeal, chopped into little bits and scattered among unrelated heaps of nonessentials. Theological investigation becomes an exercise akin to archaeology, where minute fragments of truth about God's will may be found by the patient sifter of debris. Just when we should observe the Lord's Supper, for example, shows the author's attitude and method.

The fact that the command here [Hebrews 10:25] is "incomplete," that is, that the author of Hebrews did not explain in detail the nature of the "custom" of assembling which he had in mind, is a logical implication or a necessary inference that the early Christians of that day knew the details, and were well acquainted with the complete pattern requirements.[41]

[39]Bob E. Duncan, "Reformation and Restoration," *Restoration Review*, Vol. I, No. 1, p. 38.

[40]From *We Be Brethren*, by J. D. Thomas, p. 238. Copyright 1958 by Biblical Research Press. Used by permission.

[41]*Ibid.*, p. 97.

If the early Christians knew all this and thus had every problem solved, they should have conveyed this unquestioned full program to their descendants in unmistakable terms so as to make unnecessary some 2,000 years of schism and sin. Dr. Thomas' formulas are artificial and subjective. At critical points his complex system moves on wheels of "common sense." Even the legalistic elements are not perfect. To make the word "sing" mean "sing *a cappella*" and then apply it exclusively, is a handy weapon in opposing instrumental music. But how does it do to make other New Testament teaching concerning singing exclusive? James 5:13 tells us to sing when we are cheerful. Does this make it apostasy and sinful to sing when we are sad or downhearted? Does Ephesians 5:19 mean that we are to teach one another when we sing and therefore cannot sing when by ourselves?

The final criticism is, How does this program work? We see no signs that the major reason for writing the book—to retain orphans homes and other multimillion-dollar "missionary societies by other names" at Abilene and Lubbock—means that they are now acceptable to legalistic brethren who formerly opposed them.

A historian of Disciples of Christ once looked back on their career and noted that there were forces threatening to make them "a fissiparous sect of jangling legalists." Any unprejudiced reader of the periodicals of the Churches of Christ would say that that body has gone a long way toward achieving the unhappy fate which once beleaguered Disciples of Christ.

VII

From the foregoing survey of the experience of Disciples of Christ and the Churches of Christ, we may conclude that the more specifically the restoration plea has been defined in terms of governmental, organizational, and ritualistic patterns of behavior, the less success it has had as an effective and cohesive force in the Christian world. The achievement of these two groups may in time parallel that of the Mennonites, who have produced sixteen divisions in their search for exactness in Christian organization and life.[42]

Leaders continue to appear among the Disciples, however, who become intrigued with the idea that the restoration concept can be defined in absolute, detailed terms. This is an act of wishful thinking, not of reason based on historical facts, as in the case of one of the most competent historians, when he says with keen insight:

Continuous re-definition of the plea has been made as changing conditions require. Toward the close of the 'sixties Isaac Errett published his *Synopsis,* later expanded into the famous tract, *Our Position.* This was denounced in *Lard's Quarterly* and in the *American Christian Review* as a "creed." But there was no official body to give it symbolic standing, and the cry against it fell unheeded. In succession, Walter Scott published his work *The Messiahship,* Professor Milligan his *Reason and Revelation,* and Professor Everest his *Divine Demonstration.* . . . It is significant that no Disciple has written a systematic theology. Books on the position of the Restoration Movement have been helpful—authoritative they have not been. They have won acceptance only as they have contended for liberty in exalting the Lordship of Christ.[43]

However, on page 51 of the same work an appeal is made for unity based on the "express terms or approved precedent" of the New Testament. To be sure, the author here makes this program individual-centered rather than congregationally or organizationally achieved, and further indicates that reunion "is at once ethical and mystical." This is a genuine advance over the thinking of an older generation. It is also in harmony

---

[42]This seeking after an exact pattern of outward organization is always the cause of church divisions. Principal among the barriers to union, or even to intercommunion, is the pattern-mindedness of the Anglicans and Eastern Orthodox advocates. In the official study volume used in the World Conference on Faith and Order at Lund, Sweden, in 1952 (which this writer helped to prepare), it is stated: "Thus apostolic succession is not regarded as the decisive point which constitutes a 'Church,' but as one indispensable element among a variety of others, which together make up the essential pattern of 'the Church'; . . . While non-episcopal Churches often feel that insistence upon a particular form of this 'essential pattern' is itself a distortion of the New Testament view of the Church, they do not regard this as a barrier to intercommunion. But it is on this whole question of the pattern of the Church and not on the isolated factor of valid orders that agreement must be reached if intercommunion is to be possible." *Intercommunion* (New York: Harper & Bros., 1952), p. 33. Used by permission of Student Christian Movement Press Limited.

[43]From *Adventuring for Christian Unity,* by D E. Walker, p. 39. The Berean Press.

with the basic position of the latest, book-size treatment of the "pattern" problem, Jean Louis Leuba's *New Testament Pattern*.[44]

A proposal to define the restoration plea was made by Harold W. Ford in the *Christian Standard* of February 18, 1950, His article opened by observing that "One basic problem seems to lie at the root of the troubles of the Restoration movement today. This is the problem of definition." His outline of the features of the plea includes (1) the New Testament as God's revelation. Some may have difficulty in reconciling the statement here that "The word of the apostles is to be regarded as highly and as authoritative as the word of the Lord himself" with the second requirement, namely (2) no creed but Christ. The next items are (3) the New Testament plan of salvation, (4) the New Testament Church, and (5) world evangelism. This enumeration, however, like most of its predecessors, is without any clear specification of exact definition which would distinguish it from other Christian programs. When the author concludes that the world church is ineffective through division, and triumphantly proclaims: "The Restoration Movement has the answer," the casual reader would never guess that the author is a leader in the movement which in 1955 resulted in a second separation from Disciples of Christ, a "Church of Christ Number Two" as compared with the separation of Church of Christ Number One which emerged in 1906. He is particularly opposed to having Disciples unite with American Baptists, although both are immersionists. This could honestly be termed puritanism, but should not raise the claim to being a unity enterprise.

A letter from the late Frederick D. Kershner to this writer turns the discussion into a channel unexplored to date. He says:

[44]Leuba is the pastor of the French Reformed Church in Basle, Switzerland. His book (copyright 1953 by Lutterworth Press) asks, What kind of unity does the New Testament reveal; what pattern of God's activity is therein exhibited? The reply is a twofold pattern, one emphasizing the institutional, the traditional, the particular, the other emphasizing the personal, the dynamic, the universal. His argument is: "The work of God is, on the one hand, an institution" (p. 127). "On the other hand, the work of God is expressed in the form of event. . . . But institution and event . . . are not separate nor in conflict . . ." (p. 128). He concludes, "To suppose that this unity is no longer in the process of working itself out, that it is a static, definitive achievement, would be to suppose that a synthesis has emerged which overcomes and supersedes the ecclesiastical dualism of the canonical period. Now the New Testament itself does not formulate such a synthesis" (p. 137).

There either is a norm in the New Testament, or there is not. If there is such a norm, it is either susceptible of universal recognition or it fails to function as a norm. The fact that this universal recognition has not been present among our people and we have therefore divided because of our failure to achieve universality in our fundamental views would have troubled the Campbells, but does not disturb those who are familiar with the psychology of the past half century. We know too well the part which subconscious and unconscious urges, prejudices, feelings, and all sorts of irrational motives play in the nominally rational processes of the average human being. The reign of true rationality must always remain our goal, but we must recognize the impossibility of achieving it for at least a long time to come. In the meantime we all deceive ourselves by devious methods of rationalization which add greater confusion to the picture and to our own impressions of it.[45]

It may well be from a wedding of the hard-headed common-sense philosophy, which has characterized Disciples of Christ in America, with the first science to be born in this land, the psychology of religion, that there will come a new issue in church life and organization, a Christianity true to the original purposes of the Founder of the faith. Christianity, as the common-sense philosophy sees it, is an essentially practical enterprise, having to do with character and devotion to the divine Character. Dr. Kershner's *The Religion of Christ* so defines the essence of our religion. In moments of clearest vision, leaders of Disciples of Christ have so seen the matter.[46] A letter from John Rogers to Barton W. Stone, dated March 27, 1832, breathes this very life-sustaining spirit. Among other things it says:

In my public addresses to the churches, as well as in my private interviews, I dwell much on the importance and necessity of personal reformation,—a reformation, not consisting merely in a return to the primitive order of worship in congregations, but in a return to primitive holiness of heart and life; to that purity and

---

[45]Letter dated February 27, 1940.

[46]A moving and penetrating editorial in the *Christian Standard*, May 16, 1953, breathes the pure spirit of humility and longing for essential Christianity by which alone unity at last may come. This editorial confesses failures of the restoration program among all parts of the movement, credits certain denominations with a better performance in some aspects of the faith, and concludes that the true test "is the restoration of the individual human soul to the will of God."

peaceableness, and gentleness, and goodness, and patience, and forbearance, and long suffering—to those longings after immortality; those breathings of the soul after the mind that was in Christ; to that spirit of humble, fervent, constant prayer to him whose eyes are over the righteous, and ears are open to their prayers; and that spirit of deep concern for the conversion of the world—the conversion of our neighbors and our children, which characterized the first Christians. Ah, this is the reformation we want. . . .

Following is a statement in true spiritual descent from one of the oldest documents of the Reformation of the Nineteenth Century. Written and issued separately by Thomas Campbell at an unspecified but very early date in his American experience, it is entitled *Prospectus of a Religious Reformation,* and is reprinted in *Memoirs of Elder Thomas Campbell,* by Alexander Campbell. The illustration with which Mr. Campbell climaxed his argument for unity has a strangely modern challenge. It was the reply of the Indians of the Six Nations to a missionary sent to convert them, and said:

We also have a religion which was given to our forefathers. It teaches us to be thankful for all the favors we receive, to love one another, and to be united. We never quarrel about religion. We are told you have been preaching to the white people in this place. Those people are our neighbors; we are acquainted with them. We will wait a little, to see what effect your preaching has upon them. If we find it does them good, makes them honest, and less disposed to cheat Indians, we will then consider again what you have said.

There remains, then, the problem of social psychology as applied to religion. How can these truly New Testament ideals be given enough structure to exist and perpetuate themselves as a church? Disciples of Christ, as restorationists, have arrived at that point where they have been "withdrawn from" by those ultraconservative elements which would reduce Christianity to mechanisms and verbalisms. Their future is bright as they continue to re-examine their heritage and restore the true essentials of their faith.

CHAPTER VIII

What Should Be Restored?

A restoration movement in the church or elsewhere can never wholly reconstitute the exact conditions of life that formerly obtained or the original structure of an organization within that life. This truth is observed by the learned C. Ullmann, author of the two volumes entitled *Reformers Before the Reformation.* "Reformation," he says in the introduction, "means formation again, restoration of life. In the idea, however, of a restoration of religious life, three essential elements are involved." He continues:

In the first place, it is a going back to something already fixed and original; for the Reformation, which must be distinguished from the introduction of Christianity and the first establishment

165

of the Church, aims not at the creation of some wholly new things, but at the renovation of an already existing institution. Accordingly it always proceeds upon a distinct historical domain, and in overstepping this boundary, loses its character. But then, secondly, it is not merely a return or reference to, a recognition of or longing after, an original. It is much more, an effectual restitution of it, a new and successful introduction into life of that which is ascertained to be genuine; and this mainly constitutes its practical and positive character. It is a great historical act, but one which rests upon a given foundation, clearly known and recognized in the general conscience, and which for that reason becomes in its turn the basis of a further development—a spiritual re-edification. In fine, the nature of a Reformation likewise implies a conflict with what is false, and an abolition of what is antiquated, by which its position is converted into opposition.[1]

It is on the basis of these "essential elements," and especially the second one, that Ullmann concludes that the Lutheran Reformation of the sixteenth century was "a deliberate return to primitive Christianity . . . it restores primitive Christianity to life."[2] It is possible to distinguish in abstract thought between a Reformation, such as that of Luther, and a restoration, such as Alexander Campbell proposed, and to claim that the latter means "completing the Reformation." It should be obvious to the historical observer, however, that the Campbell movement was largely affected by American and democratic aims even as the Lutheran enterprise was influenced by German and limited-monarchy ideals. Each was, in the words of Ullmann, "a great historical act," and each was essentially "a spiritual re-edification." This is why he modifies his claim about the complete restorationism of the Lutheran undertaking, "building upon the word rightly expounded, and upon the pattern of the primitive Apostolic Church cordially embraced, all faith and practice," but giving to these, he admits, a "purer and freer mould!"[3] A more succinct judgment is rendered by George La Piana, eminent former Romanist theologian, when he says of the sixteenth-

[1]C. Ullmann, op. cit., I, 1-2.
[2]Ibid., I, 3.
[3]Ibid., I, 10.

century reformers, "when they claimed that they were going back to the ancient discipline of the Church they were victims of an illusion."[4]

What church, indeed, would claim to have retained the exact mould of apostolic dress, or male suffrage, or communal sharing, or many other primitive Christian social forms, except as ideals to be adapted? If the reader of these lines is honest, he will have to admit that he cannot restore some attitudes of the New Testament in their true meaning. He adapts them, giving them a new and originally unintended significance. For example, it is clear that the earliest apostolic church was a society of the expectant. Jesus was to return, and that right soon. Paul meant exactly what he said when he wrote in the earliest book of the New Testament, to the church at Thessalonica:

For the Lord himself will descend from heaven with a cry of command, with the archangel's call, and with the sound of the trumpet of God. And the dead in Christ will rise first; then we who are alive, who are left, shall be caught up together with them in the clouds to meet the Lord in the air. (1 Thessalonians 4:16-17.)

Paul was not intending here to write a funeral manual for the year 1960; he was writing a book of instructions about how Christians should live in the first century. Every minister who reads this passage for Christian edification today is redefining the apostle's meaning in order to make it defensible. The same may be said of 2 Peter, chapter 3, and other New Testament passages.[5]

Not only is this true of the apostolic church; it is most certainly true of the Ante-Nicene church. Here we may see the process of redefinition for defense in its finest flower. Kaleido-

---

[4]"A Totalitarian Church in a Democratic State: the American Experiment," *Shane Quarterly*, April, 1949, p. 71. Used by permission of Christian Theological Seminary, publishers.

[5]See Conrad H. Moehlman, *The Church as Educator* (New York: Barnes & Noble, 1947): "The original glowing faith of the followers of Jesus was the hope of the immediate, supernatural, cataclysmic establishment of the overworldly kingdom of God upon this earth. . . . They made no blue print of ecclesiastical organization; they never dreamed of apostolic succession; they never produced a Bible of their own. . . . Why should they? Within a generation there was not going to be any evil world." (pp. 3-4.) Used by permission.

scopic change had come to the growing body of Christ. Into its membership by conversion came Justin, a pagan philosopher in search of salvation. Later, into its membership was born Origen. Today we utter with pride the names of these Christian apologists, defenders of the true faith once for all delivered to the saints.

Justin's conversion was as unlike Paul's as day is different from night. In his school he began the process of rationally defending his adopted faith. He discovered new and unexpected "meanings" in the scriptures. Origen, likewise, hearing the scoffings of learned pagans, replied to the charge that Christianity was too naïve for cultured Greeks. "It is you who are ignorant," he answered. "The true wisdom is no shallow bowl, easily drained." Thus he proceeded to create his involved and elaborate systems of allegory for the "explanation" of the scriptures.

These men loved the church. They were convinced that it was the guardian of a timeless message. For this faith Origen mutilated and emasculated himself, and Justin became Justin Martyr. In the name of Christ they breasted the new wave of Greek cultural opposition, redefined and refashioned the permanent values of the gospel message as it had come to them, and preached these truths to their own generation in terms which the people could understand.

This constant adaptation of spiritual truth into a "freer mould" of material expression may be seen to be a process by which the truth is made more clear and explicit, rather than a loss of the original ideal. C. C. Morrison's volume of Lyman Beecher Lectures of 1939, entitled *What Is Christianity*, catalogs the many schools of thought in Christian history and observes that "Each school believes itself to have discovered the 'essence' of Christianity." The historical relativity of doctrinal interpretation is asserted in his affirmation that "in every case the insistence upon the special insight of that school as the essential truth of Christianity was a reaction to a specific situation." The means of escape from this relativity in the Christian system is in seeing that "in all this conflict of Christian ideologies, there is being made some fresh disclosure of the inexhaustible riches of spirit and truth which our religion forever carries within itself."[6]

I

Now that we have made the historical survey of the working of the restoration concept in religion, we come to the major purpose of this volume, namely to discover what should be restored from the treasures of the Founder and his original institution in religious living today.

(1) *The vision of ends, or aims, or purposes, rather than any deification or ossification of means to those ends must be our first restoration objective.*[7]

Walter Marshall Horton says:

When a culture is young and full of sap, like a fresh green shoot, it is more concerned with questions of *ends and meanings* than with questions of *ways and means*. The *means* which it uses to solve the inevitable problems of food, shelter, transportation, etc., are always kept subordinate to the intrinsic *ends* of life which it envisages with deep, worshipful appreciation in its art and literature as well as in its religion. But when a culture grows old, the symptom of its incipient decay is to be seen in the thickening of its woody stalk, the growing predominance of externals and mechanisms in its life, the loss of its vital upward urge toward intrinsic and enduring values.[8]

Applying this historical truth to the present-day situation of Disciples of Christ, we may say that the passing of 149 years since the *Declaration and Address* has brought the movement

---

[6]Pages 8, 9, 10. Used by permission of the author.

[7]One does not have to adopt the whole Roman Church position in order to recognize certain truths gleaned by its advocates. For example, Alfred Loisy says, "In their warfare against tradition, the most enlightened Protestant theologians, those who, like Herr Harnack, recognize a kind of relative necessity in the Catholic development, argue none the less eagerly about it, as though it were not evident that *the desire to restore Christianity to its primitive form and organization is really a desire to condemn it to death. . . ." The Gospel and the Church*, p. 169. (Copyright 1903 by Isbister & Co.)

[8]From *Can Christianity Save Civilization?* p. 11. Copyright 1940 by Harper & Brothers. Used by permission.

to the need of a new restoration within itself.[9] The simple fact is that a recognizable segment of these people and churches is not vitally interested in unity, and refuses to accept any responsibility for Christian world leadership.[10] Others refuse to accept fellowship with those who are so concerned. Unified Promotion, the Disciple clearing house, long permitted so little money to go to their own principal unity organization, formerly called the Association for the Promotion of Christian Unity, but now termed the Council on Christian Unity, that ofttimes many workers scarcely knew it existed. However, in recent years congregations of Disciples of Christ have grown in concern for the practical, financial phase of unity work and now regularly meet their quotas in such agencies as the National Council of Churches (U. S. A.) and the World Council of Churches. In the work and leadership of these agencies, indeed, Disciples of Christ exercise an influence and are accorded a respectful attention out of proportion to their numerical strength. This is a tribute to the vitality with which concerned individuals portray the unitive tradition in their life.[11]

A means can always be found by a society to accomplish an end or aim that is a truly consuming passion of those who hold it. Any lack of a means, or at least of a constant if unsatisfied

[9]We should not be surprised at this fact. Indeed, it was predicted that this condition would come to pass. George A. Klingman says in his book, *Church History for Busy People* (p. 106), "Thus through the centuries rings the voice of 'reform,' and in our own day it is by no means silent; nor, indeed, should it be; for each generation has its peculiarities, its abuses, corruptions and innovations. The true 'reformer' has a noble mission; and as no 'reformation stays reformed' for any long period of time, there is ever the recurring need of raising the 'battlecry'—'Back to Jerusalem, back to the Bible.' "

[10]This is true of that segment of the fellowship of Disciples known as "Independents." Hoyt S. Canary says, "This brotherhood that I love has basked in the mud of mediocrity. Even if the charge angers, the charge is still true. New Testament preachers do not have a national audience; our professors are not writing books; our schools are not producing scholars; our impression on the life of the world is pathetic." *The Seminary News*, December, 1952, p. 1.

[11]For an excellent survey of achievement of Disciples of Christ in unity activities, see W. E. Garrison, *Christian Unity and Disciples of Christ* (St. Louis: Bethany Press, 1955), Chapter IX, "The Council on Christian Unity." Clearly the high watermark of recognition for contributions of the brotherhood to interchurch fraternity was the dedication of the great *History of the Ecumenical Movement, 1517-1948* (Philadelphia: The Westminster Press, 1954), edited by Ruth Rouse and Stephen C. Neill, and sponsored by the World Council of Churches, as follows:

To
THE DISCIPLES OF CHRIST
Whose untiring ecumenical spirit
has once again been manifest
in the generous provision of the funds
which have made possible the writing and publication
of this
HISTORY OF THE ECUMENICAL MOVEMENT

170

search for a means to the end, would be a stern criticism of Disciples of Christ as a unity movement. Important older books on the subject, such as Arthur J. Brown's *Unity and Missions* mention Disciples only casually. William Adams Brown's volume, *The Church in America,* says:

To-day the Disciples have become for all practical purposes a denomination among denominations, retaining as a remainder of their original motive only this: that among their various Mission Boards they have one whose sole function it is to promote the unity of the Church.[12]

These former signs of decay of the original purpose of this church movement were, as Horton suggests, due to "the thickening of its woody stalk," the preoccupation with outgrown means, to the loss of the life-giving passion.

If a more recent illustration of this loss of spirit is desired, we may cite the leading editorial in the *Christian Standard* for February 10, 1945. It affirms, "A pernicious teaching . . . is being given out to churches historically connected with the Restoration movement to the effect that this movement was started by men who had a deep passion for union." It concludes, "We are not interested in union with infidels," by which is meant Baptists, Congregationalists, and others with whom Disciples of Christ are currently seeking closer fellowship.

Giving priority to a vision of ends, aims, and purposes in our restoration program does not mean that we can dispense with concern for formal and institutional elements in the character of the church. It is with a true instinct that the Faith and Order Commission has been given a large position in the structure and work of the World Council of Churches. The church must have a visible body to operate effectively in the world. But form is always subordinate to purpose, and finds its highest good in exhibiting that intention correctly. A restoration movement that gets sidetracked into a program for the preservation of antique customs—except as those ancient customs are indis-

---

[12](New York: The Macmillan Co., 1922), p. 86.

pensable to an exhibition of the inner spirit and the discerned truth—deserves the usual fate of antiquarian societies.

II

(2) *To affirm and cultivate and enlarge the unity that already exists in the family of Christian people* must be our second restoration objective.

The situation that obtains today is closely akin to the condition Thomas Campbell met in 1809. He organized the Christian Association of Washington, Pennsylvania, to explore certain grand principles as means to church unity. As the historian of that event saw the matter:

Neither Thomas Campbell himself, however, nor those associated with him, had a full conception of all that was involved in these principles. They only felt that the religious intolerance of the times had itself become intolerable, and that a reformation was imperiously demanded.[13]

Restoration movements are themselves subject to the dangers which afflict other types of church bodies. In the case of Disciples of Christ today, as certain of the previous quotations indicate so clearly, there has grown up an intolerance for the very unity the movement originally was designed to discover through recognition of the Christian status of earnest members of the various segments of the church. Here is one of the ultimate ironies with which history occasionally confronts us, and in the presence of which the devout can only pray. The persistence of this "Independent" group in refusing to cultivate cooperation and unity measures with other Christian bodies, while the main portion of Disciples did so, led to the withdrawal of these anti-union forces into an exclusive "Church of Christ Number Two" in 1955.

Disciples of Christ are one of the free or congregational types of church which embrace the Baptist, United Church of Christ, Quaker, Universalist, and other like-governed denominations.

---

[13]Richardson, *op. cit.*, I, 245.

By historical circumstance Disciples are peculiarly related to the Baptists, and by temperament, government, and American experience they are likewise kin to the United Church of Christ. Students who are not afraid of names and facts will recognize also the close relations Disciples once enjoyed, long ago, with the Unitarians.

If Christian unity is to be anything more than an old folk tale among Disciples, practical and effective measures must always be operating to vitalize the ideal. The present times are propitious for such action. Christian unity is in the air. The failure of world governments in their search for harmony and peace is a result of the failure of the churches to lead the way in co-operation and unity. The safety of man, the preservation of civilization, and the yearning of the God of heaven call for such action.

To revive the dormant hopes and spiritual courage of the fathers of the restoration movement may mean tremulous and unstable times for the brotherhood. Progress is made when risks are taken. Faint hearts may be lost to the fraternity, but those who have the unity ideal which gave Disciples of Christ birth will carry the cause to greater victories. The patternmakers will be left to spin their intricate theories into frail ecclesiastical structures which will be divided and subdivided through the years as is the natural fruitage of their exclusiveness, their holier-than-thou religion. Unity is the fruit of a spirit, a spirit which has struggled for dominance among Disciples since the days of the founding fathers. It must be made primary or the body will descend to the limbo of curious sects.

That this spirit can scarcely be expected to emerge from the "Independent" and now-separated wing of the movement of Disciples of Christ is admitted by one of its own leaders, Howard A. Hayes, of Minnesota Bible College, in the *Restoration Herald*, November, 1953. He refers to the Independents as the "third fragment" in the following paragraph from his article:

. . . We see a divided brotherhood with a total membership of little more than three million. One segment is known for speaking where the Bible is silent, and binding as a matter of faith a

173

sectarian prejudice; a second group is led by a liberal clique into the smugness of a "respectable" middle-class denomination insisting that the means of unity is not faith, but co-operation; a third fragment shouts the old slogans and prates its "loyalty" but denies by its life the spirit of both the Restoration fathers and the New Testament; and, finally, there is a fourth element, scattered throughout the other three, which fathoms to some degree the meaning of the New Testament and the implications of the plea, and constitutes the remnant upon which the movement must depend for a resurgence of life.

Adventurous religious living in behalf of unity may have results such as came to Thomas Campbell. He began a certain communion service as a Presbyterian in good standing, but ended as only a Christian. Theodore Parker preached a sermon at West Roxbury, Massachusetts, on "The Passing and Permanent in Religion." He began as a Unitarian in full fellowship but ended outside that fraternity, belonging to the company of Christians everywhere, and remained the long-popular pulpit prince and writer of Bible commentaries. As one observer put it, he cut down all the trees in the forest of liturgy but left room for great mansions of personal and social Christian living.

One of the most serious recent attempts to assess the theological capital of Disciples and to estimate how it may be invested in the modern world for best returns is the series of lectures by the former Principal of Overdale College, James Gray, M.A., Birmingham, England, which he delivered in many of the colleges and seminaries of Disciples of Christ, in America, Australia, and New Zealand. They were published in *Shane Quarterly*, April, 1953. In his conclusion Principal Gray says:

This means that we must scrutinize our own traditions afresh in the light of the central classical normative tradition expressed in Scripture, and it means a new readiness to take a full and unreserved part in the ecumenical conversation—again at all levels and in all localities—and a new readiness to hear the Word of God in other traditions than our own.[14]

---

[14]Page 78.

174

To this the present writer is compelled to add, on the basis of personal experience, that attendance on the major theological conferences of non-Roman Christendom in this century has made one fact clear—that there is a full and generous welcome accorded every informed utterance offered by Disciple participants in the passionate search of the church today for greater unity. If Disciples really want their message to obtain a sober consideration in the most responsible quarters of Christian influence, they need only to proclaim their historic principles in the centers of theological and ecclesiastical restudy, such as the Faith and Order Commission of the World Council of Churches.

III

(3) *The modern restoration will be the recapture of the optimism and expectancy of the primitive Christian church.* The New Testament has many promises waiting to be fulfilled. It specifically affirms that the Holy Spirit shall lead the faithful into all truth. Looking the facts in the face, if Disciples in 1960 have all the truth, the Holy Spirit's promise has been greatly overrated. The failure to enjoy optimism and conquest, and to amaze the world, as did the early, spirit-moved church, is a human failure and not that of the divine Spirit.

It will be necessary for such a society to do something not always congenial to organizations, and that is to remember that the clothing and customs and outward forms of the inner faith are the creatures of a given epoch and will vanish. Harris Franklin Rall's volume, *Christianity: An Inquiry into Its Nature and Truth,* has a chapter entitled "The Finality of the Christian Religion." Rall says, "Historically the Christian religion has approved itself as final by this very capacity for growth"[15]—by the critical evaluation and sluffing off of outgrown forms, rituals, and creeds.

---

[15]Charles Scribner's Sons, 1941, p. 79. An illustration of the inevitable growth and change of even the most staid religious institutions is to be seen in Section I, Article 4 of the Columbus Platform of Reformed Judaism, which Louis Finklestein says "does not contain much to which orthodox and conservative groups can take exception." The article reads, in part: "Revelation is a continuous process, confined to no one group and to no one age. . . . The Torah, both written and oral . . . being products of historical processes, certain of its laws have lost their binding force with the passing of conditions that called them forth." Finkelstein, Ross, Brown, *The Religions of Democracy.* Copyright 1941 by The Devin-Adair Company. Used by permission

Ernest F. Scott has traced the story of the clothing of original Christianity with unintended organization and accoutrements in his volume, *The Nature of the Early Church*. Originally, he says, the church "was the creation of an ecstasy." While "it had no set order or government," from the beginning it "has identified itself with a community." It throbbed with the fresh memory of the resurrection appearances and of Pentecost and lived in anticipation of the "soon coming" of the Lord to inaugurate the kingdom which he had said was at hand. One does not "organize" such a church, even though he may be baptized into it. Such a church—the truly primitive church—cannot be restored; it could not even be perpetuated through the lifetime of those who were in it. Paul perforce became "the great architect of the church" in the apostolic age.

Eduard Schweizer, Professor of New Testament at the University of Zurich wrote in 1957 in support of this understanding of the nature of church organization. As compared to Old Testament and other formal religions' idea of "office," he says the New Testament conception is "little less than astounding." Briefly put, he says:

According to the New Testament the Church can be defined in no other way than as a sovereign sphere involving a group of persons through whom Jesus Christ himself works in the world.

The New Testament says nothing about the form this Church should assume. . . . In matters of Church orders we find great variations between the different communities mentioned.[16]

The optimism, expectancy, and freedom of true Christianity need not be lost from the new types of containers (our "earthen vessels" in the New Testament phrase). More than to any other they belong to the Christian preacher today. There is an intrinsic quality about all restorers that inevitably makes their noble aim impractical of attainment in any formal or materialistic level. The handler of holy things, such as ideas and doctrines as well as objects, begets in himself a familiarity with

---

[16]"Unity and Diversity in the New Testament Teaching Regarding the Church," *Theology Today*, January, 1957.

his materials or conceptions that induces a feeling of prophetic quality, a right to judge what is to be perpetuated or restored. After all, some priest or prophet had to be God's mouthpiece for revelation. The Bible grew at the instance of a procession of chosen and empowered but also human intermediaries.[17] Always there devolves upon the restorer the necessity of selecting what things and practices and ideas he will recover and emphasize for posterity in his religious institution. Who would claim the Campbell movement, for example, really attempts to restore the New Testament church in "doctrine, government, worship, and life" as it professes to do? Where are the prophets and speakers in tongues; where the Jerusalem community of goods; where the male superiority (as the Puritans had the courage—or effrontery—to restore)? As Cecil F. Cheverton wrote in his pamphlet, *What Do We Wish to "Restore"?*

Do we wish to exchange the garments of our twentieth century for the flowing robes of Jesus and his disciples? Would we be willing—unless we wanted to profit by the labor of others—to ask all Christians to sell their possessions and hold everything in common? Would it seem wise to desert our beautiful church buildings for services in the homes of our members, to have only such officers as served in the first organization and to follow exactly the same programs of worship?[18]

[17]The story of the preservation of this divine revelation (known academically as "Old Testament Introduction" and "New Testament Introduction") is as plain a record as history possibly can relate of how continued generations of human preservers and restorers (scribes, rabbis, Christian Fathers, Talmudic priests) have acted upon the assumption that they were verily, even if lesser, instruments in the hands of the Divine for the interpretation and correction of the sacred record. Is there a preacher worthy of the name who has not felt the sway of this heavenly leading and voiced the same from the pulpit in the presentation of his basic convictions? If evidence is requested, consider (from a multitude of cases) the instance of Origen (died 253) who tells us in his Commentary on Matthew, Vol. XV, Chapter 14, that he was seriously concerned about "the great difference in the manuscripts, due either to the negligence of the scribes, or to the ill-advised daring of some in revising what is written, or even to those who add or omit in the revision whatever seems right to them" (Pfeiffer, *Old Testament Introduction*, 1941, p. 108). In his tremendous *Hexapla*, requiring forty years of masterful labor and equal to 7,000 pages, each set up as a six-column page, "instead of giving us the pure LXX, Origen corrupted it by additions and changes made, with the help of the other Greek versions, in order to bring it into harmony with the current Hebrew text (Pfeiffer, p. 110). Yet Jerome regarded this work as the genuine LXX, *incorrupta et immaculata* (Epistle 106, to Sunnia and Fretela)! It is no wonder that Franz Delitzsch could bring out in 1920 his list of 3,000 known and verifiable textual errors or variations in the biblical record, and that S. Sperber in 1939 could begin the classification of these variations so as to show their meaning.

[18]Four-page pamphlet, in the archives of Disciples of Christ Historical Society, Nashville, Tennessee.

We pick and choose the particular things we resolve to restore, from a variety of expressions of the changing religious life of the primitive Christian communities. This is *our* exercise of the prophetic office; we look upon our work and call it good. As Cardinal Newman remarked, "All supposed returns to the past are always innovations." There is a creative quality in every restoration and, as Isaac Errett recognized, there have been many. This creative choosing of the special elements of early Christian experience which we seek to recapture makes any fixed and unchanging pattern of institutional church life impossible of re-creation. By the intrinsic quality of its restoring process, set in new circumstances of time and perception, it claims the promise of the New Testament that the Holy Spirit shall lead them into truth for their day. This is the optimism, expectancy, and freedom we inherit from primitive Christianity and possess in our earthen vessels as Christians today.

IV

(4) *The grand concept of freedom is the overarching ideal under which this divine-human enterprise is to be realized,* and this becomes our fourth restoration objective. Law is important to society for safety, sobriety, and culture, but law is the concomitant of child ethics rather than the mark of adult living. Freedom—ordered and restrained freedom, it is true, but yet freedom—is the glorious goal of mature society.[19]

It is a primary virtue of the restoration movement of Disciples of Christ that it has shown by a strong act in history that freedom based on personal loyalty to Christ, resulting in a church shorn of theological and ecclesiastical standards for the corralling and branding of its particular members can be an effective and witnessing "church" today. This fellowship group in the Body

[19]John Wycliffe Black said in an important published address, *Obligations, Opportunities and Objectives for Churches of Christ, Disciples* (Berean Press, 1935, pp. 5-6): "There is evident, in many parts of the world, a tendency to interfere with the personal rights of the individual Christian, and to fetter his liberty in self-expression and self-determination. The obligation is incumbent upon every Christian to assimilate the truth and to be able to give a reason for the hope that is within him. To his own Master, and to him alone, he stands or falls. Private judgment and the free interpretation of the Scriptures are the Christian's inherent right, and all efforts to suppress his individuality must be resisted to the uttermost. No authority may be permitted to intervene between the instructed conscience and its Lord. . . ."

178

of Christ has exhibited with a fair degree of success what one of its members, Charles Clayton Morrison, set forth as his crucial finding in his most important of many books, *The Unfinished Reformation*. He says in the summary chapter:

Our present thesis is that the inmost structure of the united church can have no formal standards of loyalty save the authority inherent in the Lordship of Christ, and that the entire subject matter of the sectarian standards must be given its place in the freedom of its fellowship.[20]

This is a far safer ground of principle upon which to erect the bounds of the church society than the beckoning to even a revised form of universal episcopate, as proposed by John Knox in *The Early Church and the Coming Great Church*.[21] Dr. Knox is right, however, in his perceptive analysis of the New Testament literature as a record of unity ever sought but realized only to a degree—as with every other generation.

John of Goch long ago saw the dangers of what he called "unevangelical legality" to the spirit of growth and adventure in Christian living. He observed, "thus to legality is opposed Evangelical freedom . . . and to a Christianity of inventions and forms, its primitive and inward spirit of freedom."[22] He traced "the fundamental distinction between Judaism and Christianity," noting "that the one is *Law* and letter, the other is *Gospel* and spirit." The tenacity of legalism in religion he demonstrated by calling attention to a Middle Age party of Passagians, who like the Judaizers of old were Christians but "observed the whole Mosaic Law, and even bound themselves to its observance by circumcision (hence called *circumcisi*)."[23] Goch then appealed to "the inward *disposition* . . . the liberty, which is the inseparable concomitant, and even the offspring, of love" as the marks of the imperishable spirit of Christianity.[24]

---

[20]Copyright 1951 by Harper & Brothers. Used by permission.
[21]P. 142.
[22]Ullmann, *op. cit.*, I, 86.
[23]*Ibid.*, I, 88.
[24]*Ibid.*, I, 89, 90.

179

Not only may we say that freedom is the philosophical or social goal of a true restoration movement, but also we may assert that life, moral life and character, is its personal ideal. Our historical survey in this volume has shown the frequent recapturing of this true insight into the essence of Christianity. For another example we may cite here the work of the much maligned and misunderstood Erasmus. Here was a man who, in a day of violence, had his own conception of what a reformation of Christianity really meant. "Erasmus was firmly convinced that Christianity was above all things something practical. . . . A true reformation, he believed, was the moral renovation of mankind, and the one need of the age was to return to that earlier, purer religion based on a real inward reverence for and imitation of Christ."[25] Thus he satirized the follies of the theologians and the vulgar travesty of religion popularized by a decadent church. By editing the New Testament ("I wish that even the weakest woman should read the Gospel," he said) he laid the foundation on which any Christian restoration movement must wait.

This truth has been repeated in recent times by Nels F. S. Ferré, in his volume *The Return to Christianity*. He insists,

Christianity must become radical. . . . Radical Christianity is simply root Christianity. Every great reform in Christianity has come from going back to the root. But the reforms have not been radical enough.

He continues with a plea for a renovation of faith that will make the Christian religion known because of its practical achievements in human service.[26]

In 1844 Robert Richardson wrote a sketch of Disciples of Christ for I. Daniel Rupp's history of denominations in the United States. Republished in the April, 1854, *Millennial Harbinger*, it says:

---

[25]Lindsay, *op. cit.*, I, 173.
[26]Copyright 1943 by Harper & Brothers. Used by permission.

One circumstance peculiar to the society deserves notice here. It is this: that its knowledge of the Christian institution, and its conformity to its requirements, have been progressive.

It would be odd to presume that progress in the discovery of the relation of institutions to life in the Christian faith ended in 1844.[27]

<h1 style="text-align:center">V</h1>

(5) *What the qualified judgment of sincere Christians can agree is essential to worship and life* becomes our fifth restoration objective. This is only to employ again the principle Alexander Campbell began to use, but which he and his successors were tempted to abandon gradually in practice. Qualified judgment is the judgment of those qualified to render opinions. "The consensus of rational opinion of all Christian scholars of whatever Church or age is the deciding factor on matters of interpretation."[28] The New Testament is supreme, and no man can add to it, affirm two exponents of this important insight, "but for an authoritative interpretation of it they (Disciple pioneers) appealed not to a single body (as in the Catholic position) but to the competent, qualified, spiritual scholarship of the church in all the ages."[29]

Discussing the third word in his book title, *Can Christianity Save Civilization?* Walter Marshall Horton says, *"Modern civilization cannot be preserved as it is, any more than it can be restored as it was, by religion or anything else."* The function of Christianity is to redeem or regenerate civilization.

The God we trust is a God who works through human instrumentalities; and the principal means whereby his spirit and power have periodically been poured forth upon Western civilization, to rescue it from incipient decay and threatened destruction, has been *the emergence of some fresh movement of moral concern and*

---

[27]For an excellent statement of how Disciples of Christ have, historically, cherished freedom along with loyalty, see the address of Reginald Bolduan before the Victoria-Tasmanian Conference, published in the *Australian Christian*, April 28, 1953, pp. 244-245.

[28]From *Discipleship in the Church,* by James Gray, p. 50 (Berean Press, 1935). Berean Press, 1935).

[29]J. Leslie Colver and Albert Williamson, *Training for Church Membership* (Berean Press, 1940), p. 28.

religious renewal amongst Christian people, which has eventually recreated the life of secular society by first recreating the life of the churches. . . . Let it be clear, then, that if we dare to speak about "Christianity" saving civilization, we put our hope in Christianity-as-it-potentially-is, Christianity-as-it-may-become.[30]

In the last analysis, there never was a one-and-only primitive Christian church. There were numerous primitive Christian churches, with greater and lesser degrees of common practice and belief, the inclusive, distinguishing feature of which was the will to do the will of Christ. By the same token, there never has been a primitive church of Disciples of Christ. Certainly Brush Run which the Campbells organized and where they held membership so long was not one. This church was established not on the confession of Matthew 16:18, but in answer to the question, "What is the meritorious cause of a sinner's acceptance with God?" and some candidates were refused admission who did not answer to suit the majority. In its early years not one in five were baptized by immersion. The early congregations organized by Barton W. Stone were, in action and life, much more akin to Methodist churches than they were like the present bodies of Disciples of Christ. Where was the primitive church of Disciples of Christ? The answer is to be found only in the will to become one. This principle of known church history of the nineteenth century may be presumed to have obtained with regard to the church life and psychology of the first century.

The endless search for qualified judgments which will enable the church to serve every new generation is the only program or process which will make it eternal rather than only timely. Lancelot Oliver, a British editor of Disciples of Christ, stated this position in the clearest words:

We have never held that a return to New Testament Christianity *and acceptance of what we think constitutes it* are necessarily one and the same thing; and at needed moments the fact has been

---

[30]pp. 4-5, 8-9. Copyright 1940 by Harper & Brothers. Used by permission.

recalled that we must ever be ready to diminish or enlarge, as further truth breaks forth from God's word.[31]

The restoration of primitive Christianity is an operation so grand in scope and so demanding in patient seeking of precious truth that Disciples of Christ may be proud even to be among the noble company of those who have engaged in this task. There is glory enough for many in its roster of heroes—just as there is for the claimants of credit for the achievement of democracy. Indeed, these two themes are intimately related. Ernest Sutherland Bates says:

Democracy did not arise out of eighteenth century political and industrial conflicts, as a momentarily popular view misconceives. Its roots are to be found in the attempted revival of primitive Christianity by the radical lower-class sects of the Protestant Reformation.[32]

The sharing of credit for the discovery of elements of true Christianity today is the same sort of problem as faced the first church in Jerusalem. Wilbur Larremore Caswell has caught the spirit of the situation in his intriguing notes entitled "An Address By Jesus' Brother," which says, in part:

We are the apostles who actually saw Jesus, and received the gospel from him. We alone can pass on to others the powers which have been divinely committed to us. Paul has seen Jesus only in a spiritual sense. We have actually seen him. We admire and love Paul, of course. But we cannot permit him to officiate at our altar. That is all. We do not see why he is so angry over our assertion of the rules of the church. For after all, rules are rules.

Now he writes that he *is* an apostle, whatever the church at Jerusalem may think about it, that he has a higher and more divine ordination than any we are able to impart, and that he is not so sure that we are the pillars of the church, as we claim to be! But he betrays by his own confession the weakness of his assertions. He makes much of the fact that he did not come to us after his conversion, but retired to Arabia, and that when after

[31]*Bible Advocate,* May 6, 1910. Italics added.
[32]Bates, *op. cit.,* p. 9.

183

three years he came here to Jerusalem, he did not trouble to seek authority for the gospel he had already been preaching, which was revealed to him by Jesus himself, and that his gospel and his apostolic commission came from no man. He admits all that we maintain. He denies that he has received the apostolic laying on of hands, the church's method of bestowing the gift of the ministry. He is a sincere man, and an indefatigable worker. He is a prophet and a teacher of a sort. But he is not an apostle in the church of God. . . .

But we must not let our obligation to him weaken our resistance to his heresies. Let us stand firmly for the faith once delivered to the saints. Jerusalem, not Antioch, must be, and remain, the Mother of the churches. We must be content with the Jesus we know, the Man of Galilee, and have none of Paul's *cosmic Christ* or *world-church*. Our Saviour must not be transformed into a Greek divinity, as Paul would have it, or a Logos, or Divine Principle, or Creative Power, or any other pagan notion into which he would evaporate our simple faith. We must make him understand that, whatever new and strange conditions may arise, whatever new opinions may delude the minds of men, we shall not alter one jot or tittle of the gospel which has been committed to us. Though we perish, though our little church perish, though we be utterly swamped by the tide of fashionable modern doctrine, in this ancient faith we shall remain steadfast. . . .[33]

VI

(6) *We must recapture a conquering spiritual life* as our sixth restoration objective. As one historian and philosopher put it, "If Christianity would go back to its origins, cleanse itself resolutely from the silt of time, and take its stand with fresh sincerity upon the personality and ideals of its founder, who could resist it?"[34]

As to organization and creed, Disciples of Christ have been blessed with a tradition and insight splendidly in harmony with the wave of the future. As George Arthur Andrews says in his book, *What Is Essential?*

[33]Copyright 1930 Christian Century Foundation. Reprinted by permission from *The Christian Century.*

[34]Will Durant, from "The Crisis in Christianity," in the *Saturday Evening Post,* August 5, 1933.

No church should demand as its basis of membership anything other than a declaration of Christian purpose and an assent to a simple covenant, promising personal allegiance to the church and brotherly regard for all its members. If all churches should agree in demanding this, and this only, the much desired day of church unity would be at hand.[35]

The living continuity of restoration zeal carries one common deposit—the will to do the will of Christ. This should be our basic ground of union. Richard Roberts perceived this truth when he said:

The path of recovery lies in an endeavour to reproduce the primitive type of Christian fellowship under the conditions of the twentieth century. . . . If there is to be a real unity it must be the unity of Christian folk in love and service.[36]

There is value in the historic and traditional insights of Disciples of Christ, in organization and practice. There is tremendous organizing value for the church in "doing things as the Apostles did them," as far as this is possible. It would be foolish, for example, to abandon the practice of believers' baptism now, just when so great a ferment is stirring the church of England and other European Christian bodies that are awaking to the basic values found in this position. The same may be said of other discoveries made by the restoration fathers which are commending themselves to earnest Christians elsewhere in our time.

The danger of Disciples of Christ is that they may make the mistake of historic Romanism which said: Wherever the correct church organization is, there is Christ and the Spirit of God. Disciples of Christ need to recapture or restore the historic insight of the birth period of Protestantism, which said: Wherever Christ's life and the spirit of God are shown, there is the Church.

---

[35]Copyright 1910 by Thomas Y. Crowell Company. Used by permission.
[36]From *The Church in the Commonwealth*, pp. 115-116. (F. A. Stokes Co., n.d.)

187

189

191